Microsoft OneDrive 2023

A Detailed Guide on Microsoft OneDrive With Virtual Illustrations | Learn the Tips, Tricks and Shortcuts and Become a Pro in Few Days.

BENEDICT BONNY

Dedication

This book is dedicated to God almighty for his grace upon my life. And also, to my dad, Boniface and my late Mum, Edith Boniface for their impact in my life.

Table of Contents

Acknowledgement

I would like to express my special thanks of gratitude to God Almighty who gave me the strength and wisdom to write this book.

My special thanks go to Michael who kept late nights to ensure that this book was a success.

Also, I would like to express my thanks to my siblings; Stella, Kingsley, Rita for their support and encouragement.
Would it be fair if I failed to recognize the impact other members of my family and friends also played in making this book a success? Definitely not. Every of there support is what motivated me and kept me going all through to finalize this project within the time frame. Any attempt at any level can't be satisfactorily completed without the support and guidance of you guys.
Then again, I am overwhelmed in all humbleness and gratefulness to acknowledge my depth to all those who have helped me to put these ideas well above the level of simplicity and into something concrete.

Introduction

In today's fast-paced digital age, it's essential to have access to your important files and documents from anywhere, anytime. That's where Microsoft OneDrive comes in. OneDrive is a cloud-based storage solution that allows you to store, share, and access your files and folders from any device, anywhere in the world.

With OneDrive, you can easily collaborate with others on projects, share documents with your team, and access your files on the go. Whether you're at home, in the office, or traveling, OneDrive makes it easy to stay connected and productive.

This e-book is designed to help you make the most of Microsoft OneDrive. Whether you're new to OneDrive or an experienced user, this book will provide you with the knowledge and skills you need to use OneDrive effectively. We'll cover everything from the basics of getting started with OneDrive to more advanced features like sharing and collaborating with others.

So, if you're ready to take your file management to the next level, let's dive into the world of Microsoft OneDrive and see how it can help you streamline your workflow and boost your productivity.

OneDrive Keyboard Shortcuts and Hotkeys

Using keyboard shortcuts is a great way to increase productivity and save time when working with OneDrive. Here are some of the most useful OneDrive keyboard shortcuts and hotkeys:

- Ctrl+N: Create a new folder

- Ctrl+Shift+N: Create a new file

- F2: Rename a file or folder

- Ctrl+C: Copy selected files or folders

- Ctrl+X: Cut selected files or folders

- Ctrl+V: Paste copied or cut files or folders

- Ctrl+Z: Undo the last action

- Ctrl+Y: Redo the last action

- Ctrl+A: Select all files or folders

- Ctrl+Shift+A: Deselect all files or folders

- Ctrl+D: Duplicate selected files or folders

- Shift+Delete: Permanently delete selected files or folders

- Ctrl+Shift+S: Save a copy of the selected file to OneDrive

- Ctrl+P: Print the selected file

These keyboard shortcuts can be used in the OneDrive web app and the OneDrive desktop app for Windows and Mac. Additionally, some of these shortcuts may vary slightly depending on the operating system or browser used.

By using these keyboard shortcuts and hotkeys, you can streamline your workflow and quickly perform common tasks in OneDrive. This can help you be more efficient and productive when working with files and folders in OneDrive.

CHAPTER ONE

Introduction to Microsoft OneDrive

What is Microsoft OneDrive?

Formerly known as SkyDrive, Microsoft OneDrive is a file hosting/cloud-storage service enabling users to share and synchronize files. Boasting an array of features and tools, OneDrive has established itself as a powerful tool for productivity and collaboration. The cloud-based platform allows users to store and access their data from anywhere, on any device, and to work with others in real time, making it an ideal choice for remote teams. This powerful storage platform offers extensive features, including automatic syncing, robust security protocols, and seamless integration with other Microsoft applications such as Word, Excel, and PowerPoint.

The Microsoft OneDrive was launched in August 2007 by Microsoft and doubled as a storage for Microsoft Office on its web interface. On access, users are open to using a storage space worth 5GB at no cost, with the option of accessing or upgrading to 100GB, 1TB, and 6TB storage space by going for each option or subscribing to Microsoft 365.

As iCloud and Google Drive are to Apple and Android devices, so is the OneDrive to Microsoft, although it (OneDrive) has existed for at least five years before the creation of the Android's and Google Drive's cloud-storage base. Over time, OneDrive has provided immense functionalities and designs, achieving usability and high reliability. From its wide range of features to support and integration of other platforms, the OneDrive is touted to possess interfaces for both web and mobile devices, collaborative editing, photo tagging, and search capabilities, which has given it that look of completeness and maturity, earning great commendations and ratings.

Beyond its impressive technical capabilities, OneDrive's user-friendly interface and intuitive design make it a standout solution in the crowded cloud storage marketplace. Whether you are an individual, a small business, or a large corporation, OneDrive provides a scalable and efficient solution to meet your data storage and collaboration needs.

How Microsoft OneDrive Works

Microsoft OneDrive operates on a highly advanced, sophisticated infrastructure that utilizes cutting-edge technologies and protocols to deliver a seamless and reliable user experience. The platform leverages a complex network of servers, load balancers, and data centers, which work together to ensure that users can access their files and documents quickly and efficiently, no matter where they are.

At the core of OneDrive's infrastructure are its synchronization protocols, which enable users to access their files from any device and seamlessly synchronize changes across all devices. This means of synchronization is accomplished through a complex system of software tools and APIs integrating OneDrive with many other applications and platforms. The integration enables users to access their files and documents from within their applications, such as Microsoft Office, without switching between different platforms or services.

In order to ensure the security and privacy of user data, OneDrive employs a robust and sophisticated encryption technology that encrypts data both during transmission and at rest. The platform utilizes industry-standard encryption protocols like SSL/TLS (Secure Sockets Layer/ Transport Layer Security) and AES (Advanced Encryption Standard) to protect user data from unauthorized access and cyber threats. OneDrive also gives users granular control over their data privacy and security settings. It allows them to set up two-factor authentication, manage permissions and access controls, and view activity logs to track who has accessed their data.

OneDrive's collaboration features are also highly advanced, enabling users to collaborate on documents and projects in real time, regardless of location. This is made possible through software tools and APIs that enable users to share files and folders with others, set up version control, and provide feedback and comments on documents. There is also co-authoring functionality supported by Microsoft OneDrive, which allows multiple users to work on the same document simultaneously, making it a highly effective tool for team-based projects.

In addition to its collaboration and synchronization features, OneDrive employs a powerful indexing and search system that enables users to quickly locate specific files and documents using various search criteria. This system utilizes machine learning algorithms and natural language processing techniques to analyze and categorize data, making it easier for users to find the files they need quickly and efficiently.

Key Features of Microsoft OneDrive

Microsoft OneDrive offers a wide range of features for individuals and businesses to securely store, access, and share their files from anywhere. OneDrive seamlessly integrates with other Microsoft applications, making it an efficient and reliable choice for those already using Microsoft products.

1. **Synchronization**

   One of the key features of OneDrive is its automatic synchronization capabilities. That is, settings and apps on desktops, laptops, tablets, and phones can be synced, providing access for Android, iOS, and macOS users to the synced files in OneDrive's folders. Also, changes made to files on one device are automatically updated on all devices connected to that OneDrive account. This feature allows users to easily access and work on their files from multiple devices without manually transferring files or worrying about version control. Android and iPhone devices with the OneDrive app can use this to upload photos, videos, and other files to the OneDrive storage cloud system. The backup option available for your files offers your images and photos quick availability on the online OneDrive folder on Windows for viewing or in any other available format of the OneDrive app.

2. **File and Folder Syncing**

   This feature is similar to that offered by Dropbox and SugarSync. Previously, the storage and syncing systems for Microsoft were separated. This time, one cloud storage service houses the online and syncing mechanisms. With this method, access has been greatly simplified instead of a difficultly processed system.

3. **Advanced Security Features**

   Another significant aspect of OneDrive is its robust security features. Microsoft employs advanced security measures such as two-factor authentication, standard data encryption, and anti-virus scanning to ensure that user data is always protected. Users can also control who can access their files, setting permissions for individual files or folders. All OneDrive plans make this feature available, although some higher plans offer more advanced features. OneDrive also complies with various data protection regulations, such as GDPR (General Data Protection Regulation), HIPAA (Health Insurance Portability and Accountability Act), and ISO 27001, making it a reliable and secure storage option for individuals and organizations.

4. Synced Collaboration

Microsoft OneDrive offers powerful collaboration tools, making it easier for teams to collaborate on files. With OneDrive, multiple users can work on the same document simultaneously. Changes made by one user are automatically updated for all other users, allowing for a more streamlined and efficient workflow. Also, OneDrive's sharing features allow users to easily share files in your OneDrive as a web link with specific people or groups, control access levels, and set expiration dates for shared files. If the file being worked on is a Microsoft Office file, you and your team can access and collaborate on the file from different web app mediums of Microsoft Word, Excel, and PowerPoint. OneDrive also allows users to track changes made to a file, ensuring that everyone involved in the collaboration process is aware of any modifications.

5. Personal Vault

The Personal Vault is that extra layer to secure your files on Microsoft OneDrive. It is a secure area within OneDrive that requires additional authentication to access. Users can store sensitive files in their Vault, ensuring they are extra secure. With the Personal Vault, access can only be granted through a multi-factor authentication system. This means of authentication can be a security code sent to your phone, email address, or authenticator app. Other systems include encryption and biometric authentication. Additionally, the Personal Vault is designed with automatic locking and sign-out features to safeguard users' files even if they forget to close the vault manually. Encryption is done by BitLocker, locally, which locks files within some period of inactivity.

Users can access their Vault from anywhere, on any device, and anytime. Whether using a desktop computer, a laptop, a tablet, or a mobile phone, they can easily open and manage their vault through the OneDrive app or the web-based interface. This seamless integration enables users to easily work and collaborate on their sensitive files while maintaining complete control over who can view, edit, or share their data.

6. Autosaving

Losing files or data has been common due to not carrying out the act of saving. With the Autosaving feature on OneDrive, there is no panic. Flies are saved automatically to the cloud as you work or collaborate on the file. Changes made are saved within seconds. The functionality of autosaving is accomplished through the implementation of advanced algorithms and state-of-the-art technologies that ensure the integrity of data, file structure, and metadata.

OneDrive's autosaving feature ensures that changes made to files are saved in the cloud as soon as they are made. This means that users no longer have to worry about manually saving their work, as OneDrive takes care of this task. Autosaving is particularly useful when working on collaborative projects where multiple users simultaneously change the document. The feature ensures that all changes are captured and synced in real time, reducing the risk of data loss or inconsistencies in the final document.

The feature can also detect and resolve conflicts that may arise when multiple users make changes to the same document simultaneously, ensuring that the final document is consistent and accurate.

7. **Two-stage File Deletion**

Unwanted files that are not needed are gotten rid of. To do this, select each file or multiple files and send them to the Recycle Bin, which temporarily stores them. For multiple files, click on the checkboxes at the front of each file. Now the two-stage deletion feature comes in when a file has been deleted accidentally or needs to be retrieved.

This initial stage allows users to recover any files that may have been accidentally deleted. Restoring files to their original location using the Recycle Bin is very much possible or they can be permanently deleted if the user determines they are no longer needed.

However, even after a file is deleted from the Recycle Bin, it is not immediately removed from the user's OneDrive account. Instead, it is moved to a second-stage deletion process designed to provide additional protection against accidental deletion.

During this second stage, the deleted file is retained in a temporary storage area for some time before permanently deleting it from the user's OneDrive account. This added layer of protection ensures that files are not permanently deleted unless the user intentionally chooses to do so.

Benefits of using Microsoft OneDrive

Microsoft OneDrive's cloud storage service gives a pointer to its numerous possible benefits. The inbuilt features and added treats by the manufacturers give exposure.

1. Easy Setup

One of the key benefits of Microsoft OneDrive is its effortless setup process. With an intuitive and user-friendly interface, users can quickly and easily set up their OneDrive account and start using it to store, share and collaborate on their files.

Whether you are an individual user or part of a team, getting started with OneDrive is a breeze. Create a Microsoft account or sign in with an existing one, and you'll be up and running in no time. Once you're signed in, you can start uploading files to OneDrive, which will be automatically synced across all your devices, allowing you to access them from anywhere. The setup process is further streamlined by OneDrive's integration with other Microsoft products, such as Office 365 and Teams. This means that if you're already using these products, you can easily link them to your OneDrive account and start collaborating with others in real time.

Microsoft OneDrive also offers an easy setup process for mobile devices. With the OneDrive mobile app, available for iOS and Android devices, users can quickly and easily access their files from their smartphones and tablets. To set up Microsoft OneDrive on a mobile device, download the app from the App Store or Google Play, sign in with your Microsoft account credentials, and start using the platform to upload, access, and share your files. You can allow OneDrive to upload photos and videos by enabling camera upload. The mobile app also features automatic photo and video backup, making it easy to back up your device's media files to the cloud.

2. Easy Accessibility to Files

The Microsoft OneDrive comes with robust and comprehensive file accessibility capabilities. Users can enjoy the experience of accessing their files and documents from any device, location, or platform and on the go.

The advanced technology behind OneDrive provides a highly reliable and secure cloud-based solution for storing and retrieving files. This state-of-the-art platform ensures that all files and documents are stored securely, and the highest security protocols are implemented to prevent unauthorized access to user data.

Also, OneDrive provides file management tools that allow users to organize their files effectively. Users can easily search and locate files, create folders, and customize their storage preferences. This algorithm-based control provides suggestions on files due to interaction with other users. OneDrive features an intuitive sharing functionality, allowing users to share their files and documents quickly.

3. Real Uptime

OneDrive is its reliable uptime, achieved through a high degree of complexity in its architecture and implementation. The system is built on top of Microsoft's Azure cloud platform, designed with high availability and fault tolerance in mind. With this, the platform can automatically detect and recover from any hardware or software failures without disrupting service to the end user. Since 2015, OneDrive can be accessed round the clock.

Also, there is the institution of a distributed architecture that spreads data across multiple servers and data centers, providing redundancy and ensuring that data is always available even if one server or data center goes offline. This approach also allows for faster access to data, as requests can be served from the nearest available server.

In order to achieve uptime with high reliability, OneDrive also employs various monitoring and alerting systems that allow Microsoft to detect and respond to any issues that may arise quickly. This proactive monitoring approach helps prevent downtime before it can occur, ensuring that users can always access their data when needed.

4. Free Storage

With a range of flexible storage plans available, OneDrive gives its users a high degree of control over their data storage needs. Different storage options are available for you, ensuring that your data is safe, secure, and accessible at all times. Whether you're an individual user or a large enterprise, OneDrive has a plan tailored to your needs.

The free storage benefit provided by OneDrive is a valuable feature that sets it apart from other cloud storage platforms. With 5GB of free storage available to all users, you can store your most important documents, photos, and videos without worrying about running out of space. And if you need more space, probably as an organization, OneDrive offers a range of affordable storage plans that can be customized to your specific needs. There is the 1TB plan available on subscription to Microsoft 365. Also, a benefit is attached to recommending the platform to another, which can see you garner up to an extra 10GB.

5. Work Offline

With Microsoft OneDrive, users can work offline. The offline work feature provides a seamless and efficient working experience by enabling access to files and folders even when an internet connection is unavailable.

This advanced solution utilizes sophisticated algorithms and caching mechanisms to ensure users can access their data without interruptions. When a user syncs their files with OneDrive, the system automatically downloads a copy of the data to their local device, which enables them to work on the files even when they are not connected to the internet. On connecting to the internet, automatic syncing of files occurs.

Also, OneDrive allows users to choose which files and folders to make available offline. This feature ensures users can optimize their storage usage by only syncing the data they need for offline work. Additionally, OneDrive automatically updates the changes to the files, ensuring that users can always access the latest data version.

The work offline feature is unique to Microsoft OneDrive as it is not a characteristic feature of other cloud storage platforms like Dropbox.

6. Extended File Sharing

Extended file sharing is available for both localized and online versions or users of Microsoft OneDrive. Through the sync client, there is the capability to share files or folders from within and outside an organization and with anonymous users. This is done with the "Share" option. On selection, users can choose who they want to share files with or send already copied links through email.

7. Sharing Services with Encrypted Security

Most organizations harness the file-sharing feature available on OneDrive due to collaboration on documents or providing customer information. The share feature comes with a lot of flexibility with which administrators can determine the level of accessibility to already stored documents. The wrong sharing of sensitive information or documents is curtailed. Some access to documents is limited to time, and restriction sets in when it elapses.

OneDrive encrypts files stored to prevent attacks. This is a means to ensure that data is safe, stored, or shared.

8. **Document Management**

OneDrive provides an efficient document management system for users collaborating on a work or file. Although different edits, changes, and versions of work can be recorded, users are left with no worries. All changes are added to the same document with indications of the type of edits and changes made. Remote work has never been made easier.

Disadvantages of the Microsoft OneDrive

As opposed to the numerous benefits, there are some disadvantages to using Microsoft OneDrive:

1. **Error from Usage**

A common error amongst users is deleting files or documents from the computer with the thinking such files will be on the cloud as a form of backup. That is not how it works, as the syncing feature shows that deleting files from your computer within OneDrive will completely remove the file from the OneDrive cloud. Not only that, files will be removed from other synced devices.

2. **Insufficient Storage Limitations**

Microsoft OneDrive offers different plans and storage capacities, including 5 GB for a free account, which is insufficient for many users. While OneDrive provides additional storage for a fee, it may not be an economical solution for many individuals, particularly those already using different cloud storage services.

3. **Limited File Size Upload**

Another significant disadvantage of OneDrive is its limited file size upload, which is restricted to 250 GB for each file. Although this might be sufficient for most users, it might not meet the requirements of heavy data users, such as photographers or videographers, who deal with more massive files.

4. **Potential Security Risks**

OneDrive had encountered security concerns, particularly in 2016, when Microsoft revealed that it had unintentionally allowed unauthorized access to some users' files. While Microsoft has improved its security measures, OneDrive's security is still a concern for some individuals, particularly those dealing with sensitive information.

5. Issues with Syncing

OneDrive may experience difficulties syncing, resulting in data loss or corrupted files. Additionally, synchronizing large data files may take an extended period, which might inconvenience users. There is a limit to the number of files that can be synchronized. Trying to synchronize more than 300,000 files will prove difficult, and users experience low performance at a threshold of 100,000 files.

6. Limited Integration with Other Applications

OneDrive integration with other applications is limited. For example, it may not work seamlessly with some third-party applications, such as Adobe Photoshop or Lightroom, widely used in the creative industry. This limitation can result in additional effort and time spent integrating files with these applications.

Comparisons Between Microsoft OneDrive and SharePoint, and When to Make Use of Them

Regarding cloud-based collaboration and data management solutions, Microsoft OneDrive and SharePoint are two of the most popular offerings in the market. Although both platforms are developed and maintained by Microsoft, they serve distinct purposes and cater to different use cases with unique features and functionalities.

OneDrive, for instance, is primarily designed as a personal storage solution, enabling users to store and access files, documents, photos, and other digital content from any device, anywhere, and at any time. It also offers advanced features such as version control, automatic file syncing, and backup and recovery, making it an ideal solution for individual users or small teams who require basic document management and sharing capabilities. On the other hand, SharePoint is a robust collaboration platform that provides a broader range of capabilities and services, including document management, team sites, workflow automation, and business intelligence. It facilitates team collaboration and knowledge sharing, providing a centralized platform for users to store, organize, and access files and other data in a shared environment. Also, SharePoint offers advanced features such as content search, access control, and auditing, making it an ideal solution for medium to large-sized organizations with complex information management requirements.

One of the key differences between OneDrive and SharePoint lies in their scope and scale. Microsoft OneDrive is best suited for personal or small-scale use cases, whereas SharePoint is designed to handle enterprise-level needs. While both platforms offer file-sharing capabilities, OneDrive limits the number of users who can access and edit files simultaneously. In contrast, SharePoint allows multiple users to collaborate on the same file, providing a robust collaboration experience.

Another major difference between the two platforms is their pricing and licensing models. OneDrive is available as part of the Office 365 suite, which provides a range of personal and business plans with varying features and pricing options. SharePoint is typically licensed as part of the larger Microsoft 365 suite, which includes a comprehensive set of collaboration and productivity tools for businesses of all sizes.

The user interface for OneDrive and SharePoint is similar in many ways, as both platforms use a modern, web-based interface. However, SharePoint has more features and capabilities, which can make its interface more complex and potentially more challenging to navigate than OneDrive. SharePoint includes more customizable options, enabling businesses to tailor the user interface to their needs.

Although OneDrive and SharePoint access files and data from anywhere, using a web browser or mobile device, SharePoint offers advanced security features like role-based access control, information rights management, and data loss prevention. SharePoint also includes more extensive auditing and compliance reporting capabilities, which can be critical for organizations that require strict security and regulatory compliance.

Choosing between the two platforms depends on your organization's unique requirements, size, and budget, and it's important to carefully evaluate your options before deciding.

Comparisons Between Google Drive and OneDrive

Microsoft OneDrive and Google Drive are two of the world's most widely used cloud storage solutions. While both platforms share some similarities, several key differences may impact the best fit for you. Both offer a range of features allowing users to store and share files, create and edit documents, and collaborate with others in real time. However, there are several differences in how these features are implemented. OneDrive, for instance, is deeply integrated with Microsoft Office, meaning users can create and edit Word, Excel, and PowerPoint files directly from the platform. It also provides advanced security features such as ransomware detection and recovery, which helps users protect their data from cyber threats.

On the other hand, Google Drive provides users with a wide range of productivity tools such as Google Docs, Sheets, and Slides. It also offers advanced collaboration features, allowing multiple users to work on the same document simultaneously. Its AI-powered search functionality makes it easy to find files and folders quickly.

Pricing is a critical factor when choosing between Microsoft OneDrive and Google Drive. Both platforms offer free and paid plans, but the cost of these plans can vary significantly depending on your needs. OneDrive, for example, offers 5GB of storage for free, which is lower than Google Drive's 15GB of free storage. However, OneDrive's paid plans are generally cheaper than Google Drive's. The OneDrive standalone plan starts at $1.99 monthly for 100GB of storage, while Google Drive's equivalent plan starts at $1.99 for 100GB of storage. However, Google Drive's G Suite plan is more expensive, starting at $6 per monthly user.

Another consideration is performance. Both platforms offer fast and reliable performance, but there are some differences in handling certain tasks. For instance, OneDrive is better suited for users who need to work with large files or folders. It provides users with advanced syncing functionality, which ensures that files and folders are updated in real-time. It also supports differential syncing, meaning only the changes made to a file are synced, not the entire file. Google Drive, on the other hand, is better suited for users who need to collaborate with others in real time. It provides users with advanced version control features, which make it easy to see who made changes to a document and when. Users can also add comments and suggestions to documents, making it easy to collaborate with others.

Pricing of the Microsoft OneDrive

OneDrive offers a variety of pricing plans that cater to the diverse needs of users, ranging from individuals to large organizations.

For individual users, OneDrive offers a free plan that includes 5GB of storage, perfect for users with basic storage needs. The next pricing plan is the OneDrive Standalone plan, which starts at $1.99 monthly or $19.99 per year and offers 100GB of storage. This plan is ideal for users who need more storage space for personal or business use. There is also a $69.99 yearly Microsoft 365 Personal plan with 1TB of storage space, and the Microsoft 365 Family plan at $99.99 per year still at 1TB but for six different users, making 6TB in total for that plan alone.

For organizations or enterprises, Microsoft offers OneDrive for Business, which is available as a standalone service or as part of the Microsoft 365 suite. OneDrive for Business provides users with secure file-sharing and collaboration tools that can be accessed from anywhere. It also comes with multifactor authentication, compliance standards, auditing, and the ability to make reports. Pricing for OneDrive for Business varies depending on the number of users and storage requirements. For organizations with up to 300 users, Microsoft offers the Microsoft 365 Business Basic plan, which includes OneDrive for Business/ Business Plan 1, starting at $5 per user per month. This plan includes 1TB of storage per user and other Microsoft 365 apps such as Word, Excel, and PowerPoint. The Business Plan 2 is available at $10 per user per month; the Microsoft 365 Business Basic is a $6 per user per month plan, while the Business Standard costs $12.50 per month.

For larger organizations with more than 300 users, Microsoft offers the Microsoft 365 Enterprise plans: F3, E3, and E5 at costs of $8, $36, and $57 respectively with the inclusion of OneDrive for Business, and advanced security and compliance features. Pricing for these plans is based on the number of users and specific needs of the organization.

CHAPTER TWO

Setting up OneDrive Account

Access to the features of Microsoft OneDrive comes with first creating and setting up an account. At the creation of one, you now have your own OneDrive storage space.

Downloading/Installation of Microsoft OneDrive

For Windows versions 8.1 and above, OneDrive has already been installed on your computer. There is no need to go further in downloading/installing it.

- If there is no Microsoft OneDrive installed on your computer, visit the download website for Microsoft OneDrive (https://onedrive.live.com/about/en-us/download/ using your computer).

- Click the **Download** button to get the download started.

- Once the download is completed, locate the file in your downloads folder. Click on the file to begin the installation.

- Use the **on-screen prompts** to serve as a guide in installing the Microsoft OneDrive on your computer.

- When prompted to sign in, make use of your Microsoft account information. If you do not possess a Microsoft account, you can create one.

- After installation, **sign in** and get access to your files.

Creating a Microsoft OneDrive Account

To create a Microsoft OneDrive account for your Windows (version 10 especially), macOS, iPhone, and Android devices, you will need to have a Microsoft account. Already have an account on Outlook, Live, Hotmail, or that for Xbox network? Then you already have a Microsoft account and can sign in to the cloud storage service. If you do not have a Microsoft account, you can create one using the Microsoft Sign-up page.

To create a Microsoft OneDrive account:

- Go to the Sign-up page (https://www.microsoft.com/en/microsoft-365/onedrive/online-cloud-storage?ocid=oo_support_mix_marvel_ups_support_smconedrive_inline&rtc=1)

- Click on **Create free account**.

- Enter your **email address** which can be an existing email from another service such as Gmail. There is no need to try to get a new email address.

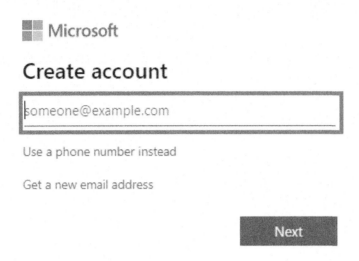

- If you do not have one, click the **Get a new email address**.

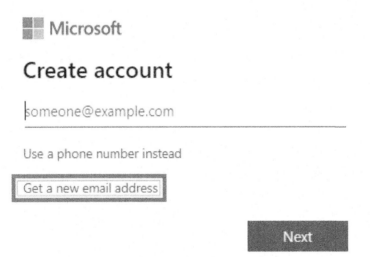

- There is also a **Use a phone number instead** option. On using that option, you will get a code through that number which you need to input to proceed.

- After entering your email address, click **Next**.

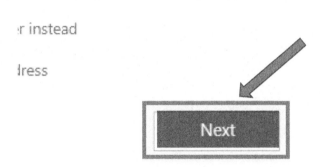

- Type in your preferred password. Click **Next**.

- Input your name, both **first and last names**, then, **Next**.

What's your name?

We need just a little more info to set up your
account.

First name
_____

Last name
_____

- This is followed by your **country and date of birth**. Click **Next**.

What's your birthdate?

If a child uses this device, select their date of birth to
create a child account.

Country/region

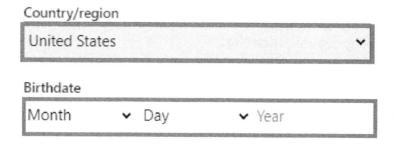

United States ⌄

Birthdate

Month ⌄   Day ⌄   Year

- An email will be sent to you containing a verification code. This is to verify the authenticity of the email address provided. Input the **code** and click **Next**.

- Add security information. You will provide your phone number as an extra layer of security. Enter the code. Proceed further, and input the captcha code.

- Finally, create your Microsoft OneDrive account.

Signing in to Microsoft OneDrive Account

- Go to OneDrive website (https://onedrive.live.com/about/en-us/signin/)

- Input your **email address or phone number** for your Microsoft account. Click **Next**.

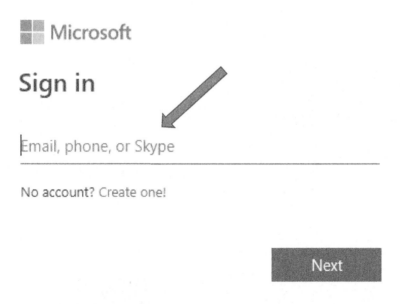

- Input password.

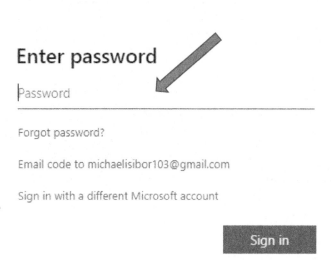

- Click on **Sign in**.

Setting Up OneDrive on Windows

A Microsoft account allows you access to an automatically configured OneDrive. This is on using the account to create a system account. Configuration is to be manually done when using an entirely new account.

- Click on the Start menu icon at the bottom left corner.

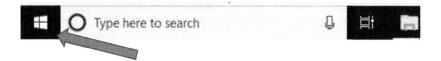

- With the search bar, look for Microsoft OneDrive.

- Click on the OneDrive app.

- This will display a welcome screen requiring you to sign in to your Microsoft account.

- Enter your **password**. **Sign in**.

- Next, choose the folder where you want to store your OneDrive files. You can either choose the default location or select a custom location.

Microsoft OneDrive   ✕

Your OneDrive folder

Add files to your OneDrive folder so you can access them from other devices and still have them on this PC.

Your OneDrive folder is here

C:\Users\dell\OneDrive

Change location

Next

- OneDrive will then start syncing your files to your computer. This may take some time, depending on the data you have stored in OneDrive.

- Once the sync is complete, you can use OneDrive to access and manage your files.

- By default, OneDrive will automatically sync any changes you make to your files. If you want to adjust the sync settings, right-click the OneDrive icon in the **taskbar** and select **Settings**.

- In the Settings menu, you can choose which folders to sync, change the location of your OneDrive folder, and adjust other settings related to file syncing.

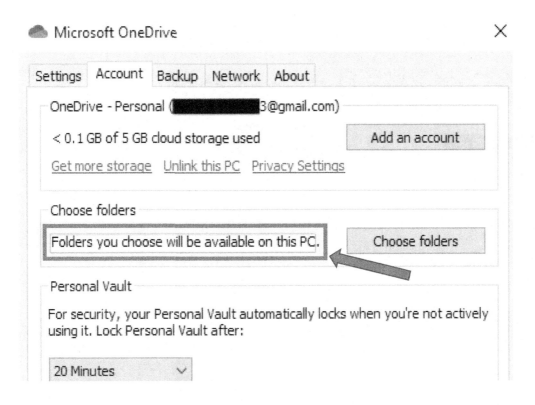

The OneDrive Interface

The OneDrive interface offers a user-friendly experience allowing users to easily access and manage their stored files. It presents a clean and intuitive design with an array of tools and features to help users interact with their files. Users can upload, create, and organize their files from the dashboard in various ways. The interface also provides options for sharing files with others, collaborating on documents, and accessing previous file versions.

One of the most notable features of the OneDrive interface is the advanced search function that allows users to quickly and easily locate specific files based on keywords or other search criteria. Additionally, the interface offers a range of customization options, including the ability to adjust the layout and design of the dashboard to suit individual preferences and needs.

The OneDrive interface is also highly secure, with built-in encryption and other advanced security features that ensure the protection of user data. This includes setting up two-factor authentication and other access controls to limit who can access the user's files.

When you sign in to OneDrive, you'll see a home page that displays your most recent files and folders. You can click on any of these items to open or edit them.

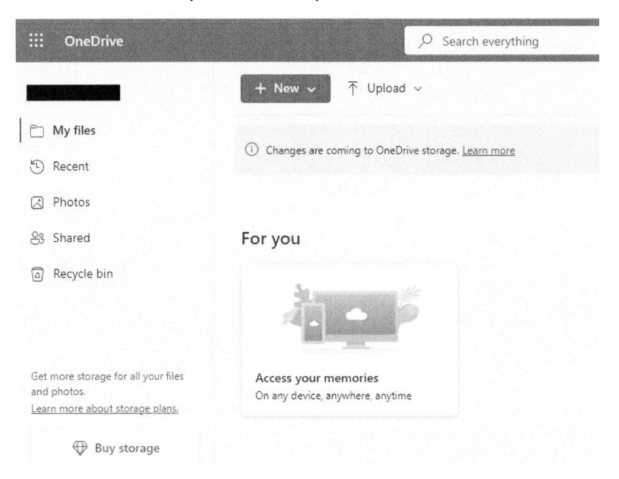

On the left side of the screen, you'll see a navigation pane that allows you to switch between different areas of OneDrive, including Files, Recent, Photos, and Shared.

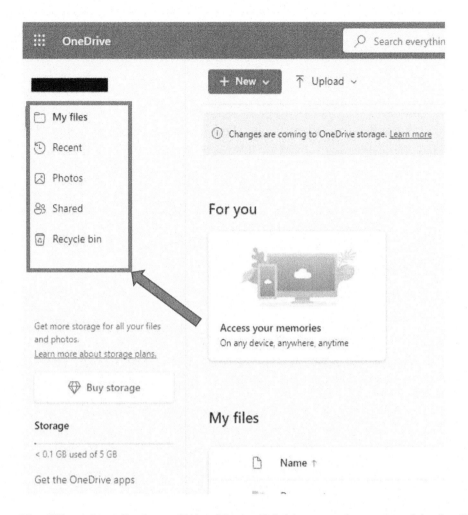

- The **Files view** displays all the files and folders you have stored in OneDrive. You can sort and filter the files by name, date, file type, and size. You can also create new folders, upload new files, and move, copy, or delete existing files.

- The **Recent view** displays a list of all the files you have recently opened, edited in OneDrive, or accessed by someone else. This provides valuable insight into the status of shared projects and can help users stay on top of important deadlines.

- The **Photos view** is designed specifically for viewing and organizing photos. You can view your photos in a grid or slideshow format and organize them into albums or add tags to make them easier to find.

- The **Shared view** shows files and folders that others have shared with you. You can view and edit these files just as you would any other files in OneDrive.

- **Recycle Bin** displays files deleted from the user's storage allowing users to recover accidentally deleted files or free up storage space by permanently deleting unwanted files.

- **Files On-Demand** shows files available in the user's OneDrive storage but not necessarily downloaded onto their device. This helps save storage space on the user's device while providing quick access to all their files.

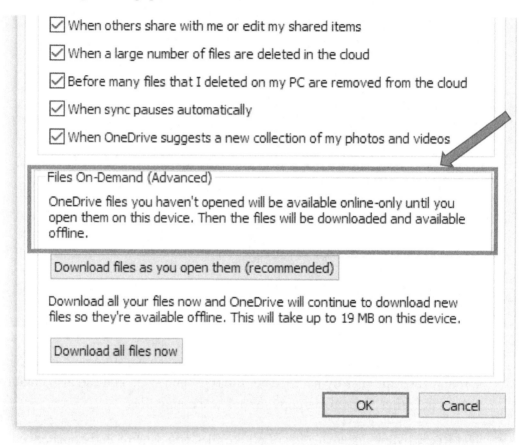

- **Offline files** show files saved for offline access using the Always keep on this device option from the Windows interface, meaning they can be accessed even without an internet connection. This is a useful feature for users who need to access their files while traveling or in areas with poor connectivity.

- **Tags** using OneDrive allows users to add tags to their files to help categorize and organize them. The tags display provides an at-a-glance view of all files with a particular tag, making it easy to quickly find files with similar characteristics.

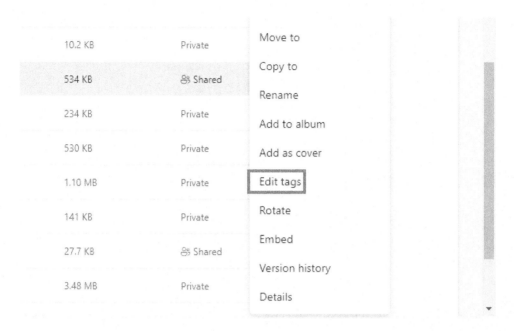

- **Shared with/by you** which shows files and folders that the user has shared with others. This makes it easy to keep track of shared projects and ensures collaborators have access to the most up-to-date versions of documents.

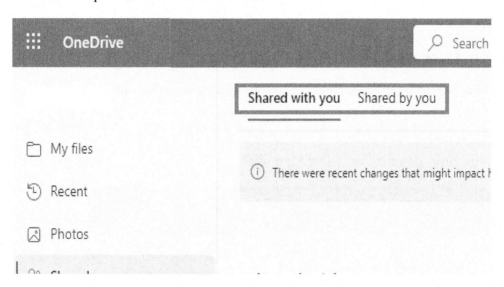

- **Storage** which shows the amount of space used and available and a breakdown of which types of files take up the most space. This lets users quickly identify and delete unnecessary files, freeing space for new projects.

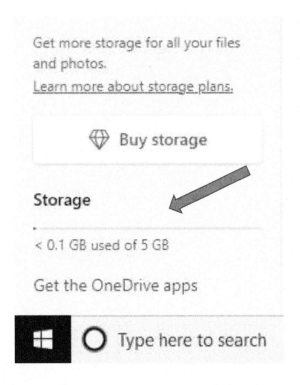

Get more storage for all your files and photos.

Learn more about storage plans.

⬦ Buy storage

Storage

< 0.1 GB used of 5 GB

Get the OneDrive apps

⊞ ○ Type here to search

Signing Out of Microsoft OneDrive

- Open your web browser and go to the **OneDrive website** (https://onedrive.live.com).

- Click on your **profile picture** or initials at the upper-right corner of the screen.

- In the drop-down menu, select **Sign out**.

- You will be redirected to the OneDrive sign-in page. Confirm that you have been signed out by ensuring you see the sign-in page, not your OneDrive files.

To sign out (unlink) of Microsoft OneDrive in Windows 10

- Locate the **OneDrive icon** on the system tray. Right-click on it to open the flyout. Go to **Settings**. Clicking on Settings opens up the OneDrive settings dialog.

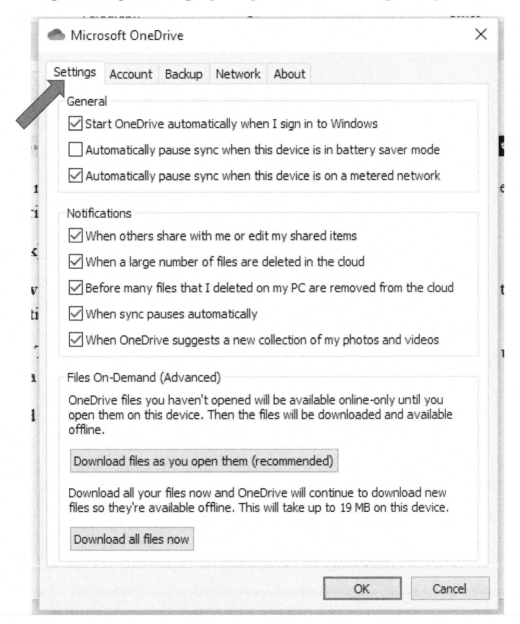

- Click on **Accounts**. You will see **Unlink this PC**. Click on this option. After the unlink, you will be shown a Welcome screen with the option to sign in.

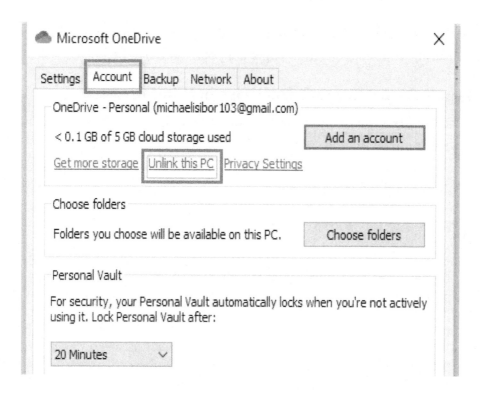

- You are now **signed out** of OneDrive using windows.

Configuring OneDrive Settings

To configure OneDrive settings, follow these steps:

- Sign in to **OneDrive**.

- Choose your OneDrive folder location: By default, OneDrive creates a folder in your user profile directory. You can change this folder location to a different folder or drive.

- Choose which files and folders to sync: You can sync all files and folders in your OneDrive or only specific ones. To do this, right-click the OneDrive icon in the system tray and select **Settings**. In the **Account** tab, click **Choose folders** and select the folders you want to sync.

- Change OneDrive settings: To change other OneDrive settings, such as the bandwidth usage or notification preferences, right-click the **OneDrive icon** in the system tray and select **Settings**.

- Manage sharing settings: OneDrive allows you to share files and folders with others. To manage sharing settings, go to the OneDrive website and select the file or folder you want to share. Click the **Share** button at the top of the page or simply hover the indicator on the file and locate the share option. Choose who you want to share with and what permissions they have.

CHAPTER THREE
Microsoft OneDrive Basic Operations

OneDrive offers an unparalleled experience that can simplify your life and enhance your productivity. Whether you are looking to save your files on the go, collaborate with colleagues, or protect your data from loss or theft, OneDrive has got you covered.

Creating Folders and Documents in Microsoft OneDrive

- Log in to your OneDrive account using your Microsoft account credentials.

- Once logged in, click on the '**New**' button at the top of the page.

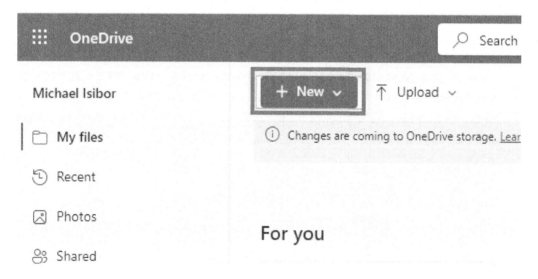

- Select **Folder** from the drop-down menu to create a new folder.

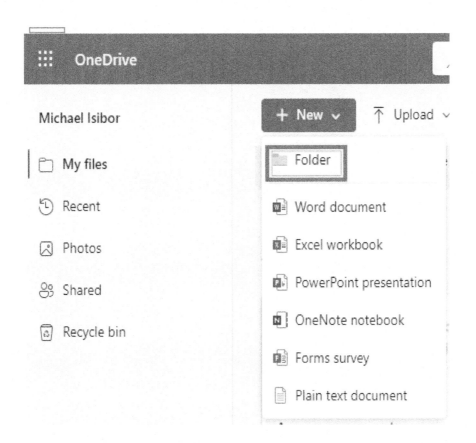

- Give your new folder a name and click **Create**.

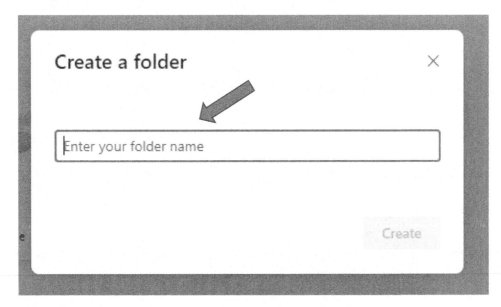

- Select the desired files and drag them into the folder.

- To create a document (file), click the '**New**' button again and select the type of document you want to create, such as Word, Excel, PowerPoint, or OneNote.

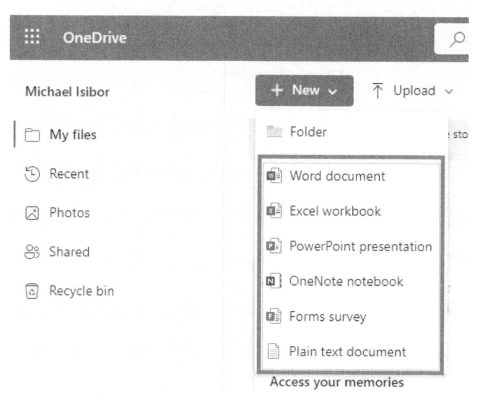

- Once you have selected the type of document, a new document will open in your browser, and you can start working on it.

- All changes are automatically saved in the Office online apps, so when you return to OneDrive, your new file is already saved.

You can also create Microsoft OneDrive folders on your computer starting from File Explorer.

In order to create a new folder:

- Click the button on the ribbon with '**New**' folder.

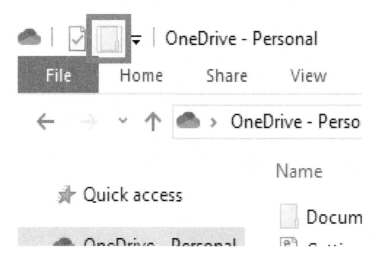

- Or right-click on the folder region. Go to **New**, and then to **Folder**.

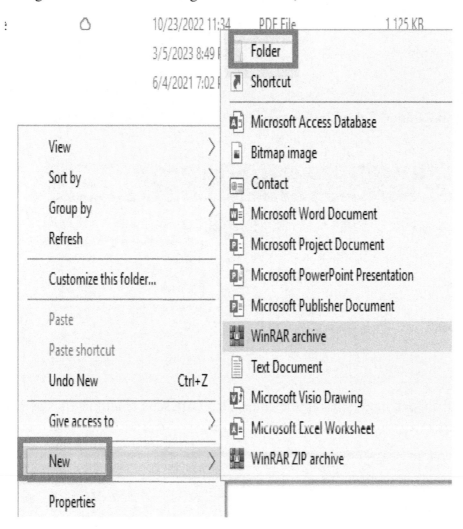

Adding/Uploading files to OneDrive on the Web

- Log in to your Microsoft OneDrive account through the web.

- Click the **Upload** button at the top of the page or in the toolbar, depending on your version of OneDrive.

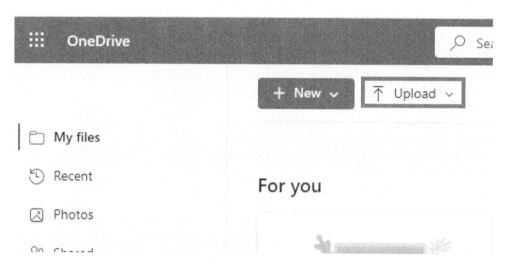

- Click **file/ folder**. Select the file you want to upload from your computer by clicking on it.

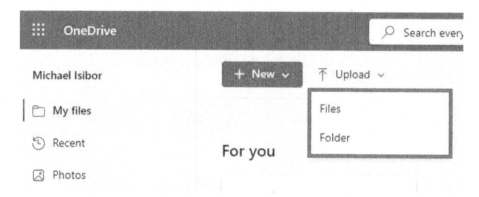

- Click the **Open** button to start the upload. You can select multiple files by holding down the **Ctrl** key.

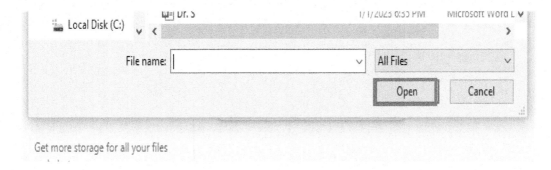

Get more storage for all your files

- The file will then begin uploading to your OneDrive account. Once the upload is complete, you can access the file on any device connected to your OneDrive account.

Uploading Documents and other Files to OneDrive on Windows

- Go to File Explorer

- Open the OneDrive seen on the left pane.

- Tap on the **Windows key + left arrow**. This will snap the OneDrive folder towards the left.

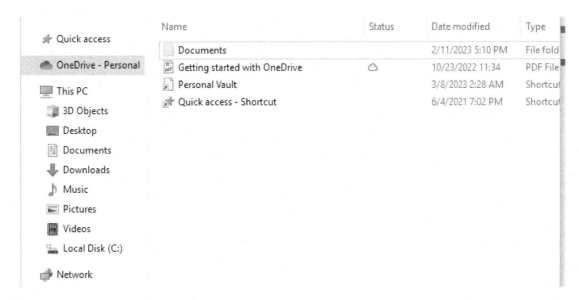

- With the **Windows key + E**, open another File Explorer interface.

- Move to the folder containing the contents to be uploaded.

- Use the **Windows key** + **right arrow** to snap the current interface to the right.

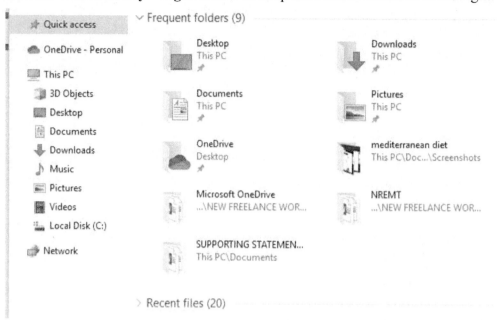

- Drag and drop contents to the OneDrive folder on the left to start the upload.

- After completing these steps, the files and folders will be automatically synced to the cloud.

Downloading Files from OneDrive

- Sign in to your OneDrive account using your Microsoft account.

- Locate the file or folder you want to download. You can use the search bar or navigate through your files and folders.

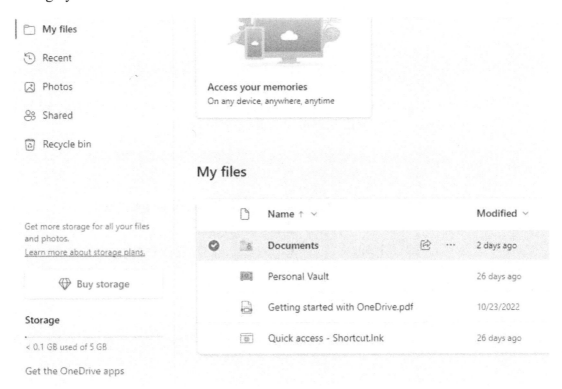

- To download a single file, **click on it** to select it. To download multiple files or an entire folder, hold down the **Shift** key and click on each item you want to download.

- If the download is for all files or folders seen in the current window, press **Ctrl + A** using the keyboard to pick files simultaneously.

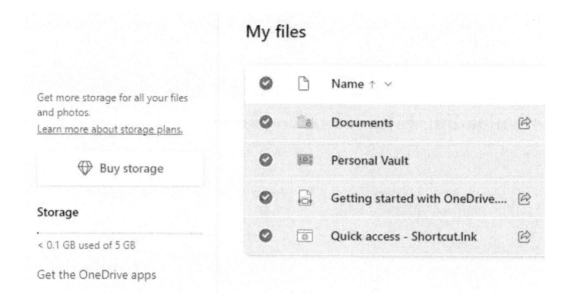

My files

		Name ↑ ∨	
✓	🗋		
✓	📄	Documents	➦
✓	▦	Personal Vault	
✓	🗎	Getting started with OneDrive....	➦
✓	◻	Quick access - Shortcut.lnk	➦

Get more storage for all your files and photos.
Learn more about storage plans.

◈ Buy storage

Storage

< 0.1 GB used of 5 GB

Get the OneDrive apps

- Once you've selected the files you want to download, click the **Download** button at the top of the page. This will initiate the download process.

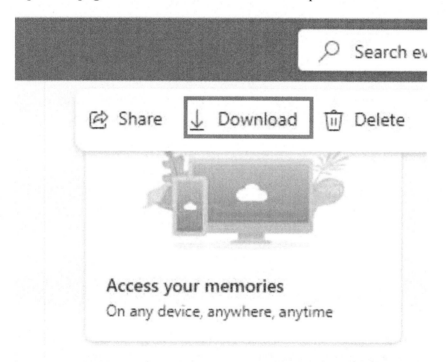

- Depending on your browser and settings, you may be prompted to choose a download location, or the file may automatically save to your default download folder.

- After the download, you can access the files on your computer and use them as needed.

- If you are using the OneDrive desktop application on your computer, you can also download files by simply navigating to the folder where the file is located and copying it to your local computer. The file will automatically sync to your computer, allowing you to access it even when you are offline.

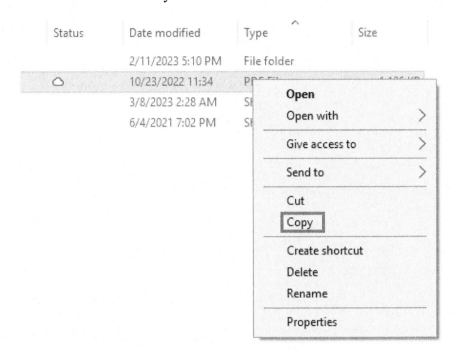

Managing and Organizing Your Data on OneDrive

On making use of Microsoft OneDrive over time, difficulties may arise with monitoring or keeping appropriate track of files. The Microsoft OneDrive comes with features to give you that edge in managing and organizing your files.

Sorting Files

Your files and folders are visible on the OneDrive page. You can choose files to view by coursing through the different options on the left plane.

The View options icon can change how you want files to be arranged. You can view your files using the following:

- **List view** allows viewing of files with names and some other details. It is more of a default view for your files.

- **Tiles view,** which shows files in a grid format.

- **Photo view** is best applied for folders with photos. Photos usually come as thumbnails presented in a grid.

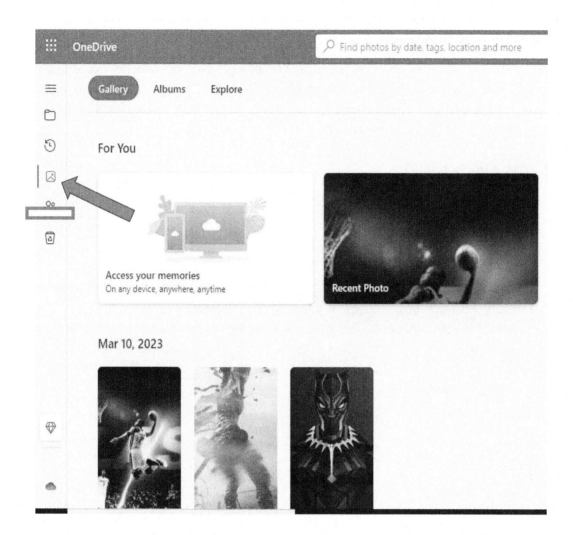

Searching for Files

Looking for files comes easily with the search feature. With search, you are directed to that particular document or file using words related to the file's title. To use the search feature, go to the **search bar**. Input the words associated with what is being searched for, then click Enter. The result of search will then appear.

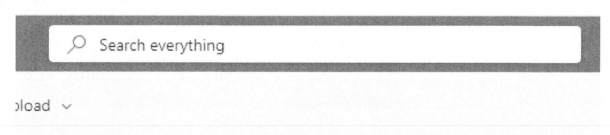

Working with Folders

Folders are a good means to organize files. You can get your documents stored and moved from one folder to another. In the process of sharing documents, folders can be quite useful. Documents moved to a particular folder, such as a shared folder, are prepared for sharing, especially when working with others.

To move a file to folder:

- Select files to be moved by clicking on the check box. This can easily be seen by hovering over the file.

- From the pop-up menu, click on **Move to**.

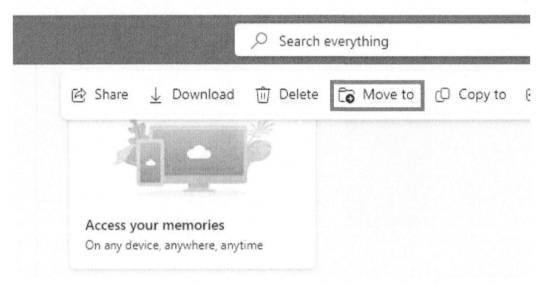

- You will see a window to select the folder. Pick the folder for the file intending to be moved. Finally, click **Move here**.

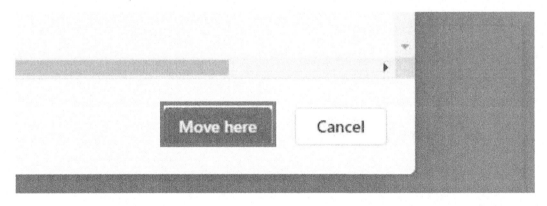

Other File Options

Other options for file management can be accessed. Right-click on the file and get to see:

- **Download**: access to the file saved as a copy on your computer. Already downloaded documents will not be updated with any form of changes made on OneDrive.

- **Rename**: giving another name to a file.

- **Delete**: taking off files that move them to the Recycle Bin.

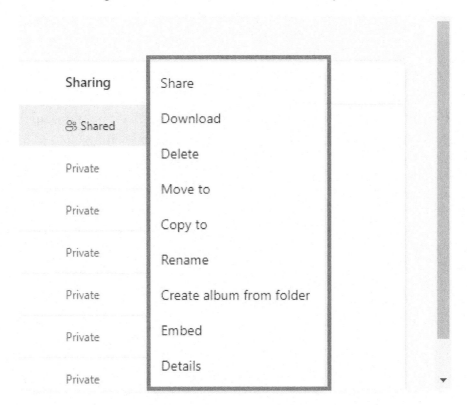

Searching for Saved Files in OneDrive Cloud

- Log in to your OneDrive account on the web.

- Once logged in, you will see a search bar at the top of the screen.

- Type in the name of the file you are looking for or any keywords related to the file.

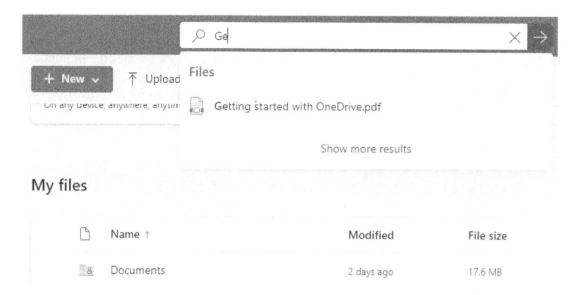

- OneDrive will display files or folders that match your search terms. You can then click on the file to open it or click on the folder to see the contents within.

If you still can't find the file you are looking for, try refining your search using more specific **keywords or filters**, such as file type, date modified, or location.

On Windows, you can search for saved files in OneDrive using the search bar in the Windows File Explorer. Here's how to do it:

- Open File Explorer on your computer.

- On the left-hand side of the screen, click on OneDrive to view your OneDrive files and folders.

- In the search box at the top-right corner of the File Explorer window, type in the file name or any keywords related to the file you want to search for.

- As you type, Windows will automatically begin to search for matching files in your OneDrive folder.

- Once the search is complete, you will see a list of matching files in the main window.

- Click on the file to open it, or right-click to see more options, such as copying, moving, or renaming it.

- If you still can't find the file you are looking for, try refining your search using more specific keywords or filters, such as file type, date modified, or location.

Sharing Files and Folders with Others (and Via Links)

Microsoft OneDrive provides a means of sharing files through anonymous link sharing to anyone or through specific targets.

You can share links containing information with virtually everyone using the share link option. Such links can be included in social media postings and newsletters. Information contained in such links can be viewed and edited depending on the permission settings.

To get access to the OneDrive sharing link:

- Select the file to be shared. This can include multiple files, which can be shared simultaneously.

- On selection, **Right-click** on the file selected and click the **Share** option as seen in the menu. The Share button can also be seen at the top.

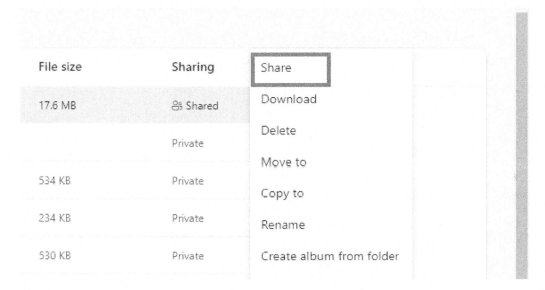

- What will appear is the **Send Link** dialog box. It comes with a default **Anyone with the link can edit** setting. If that is the right option, then proceed to the next step.

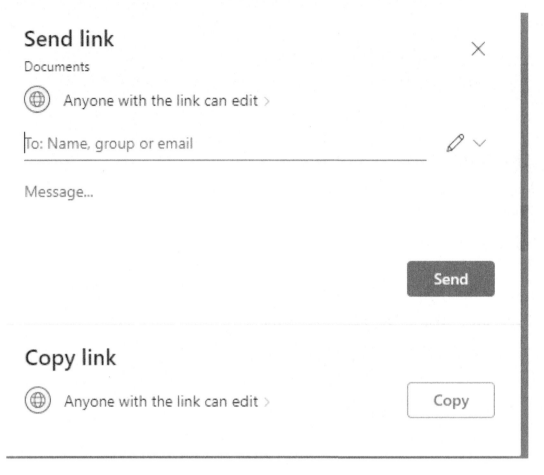

- There are other options– click on the default and configure according to what you require, under other settings. Click on **Apply** when you are done.

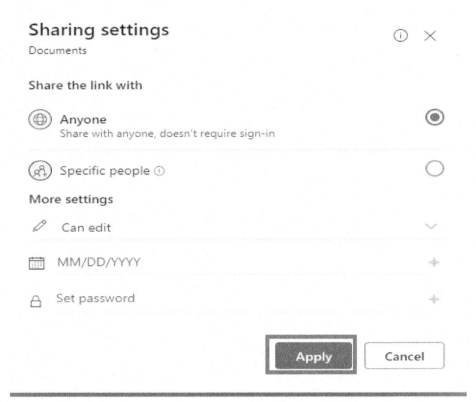

- You will be taken back to the dialog box. Click **Copy**.

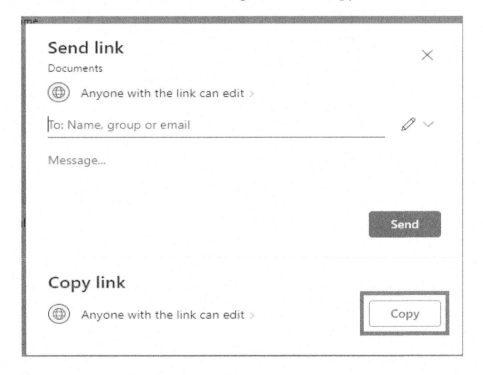

- This action copies your link to the clipboard, allowing you to share or paste links on emails, websites, or other means.

As said earlier, you can share links to specific people or targets in order to keep firm control of such information. To do this:

- After selecting the files, access the **Share** button at the top of the page or Right-clicking on the files.

- From the dialog box, click on **Anyone with the link can edit** this time around. Select the **Specific people** option.

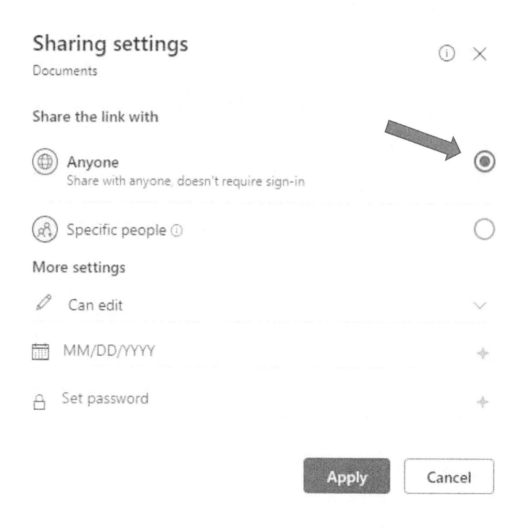

- This is followed by the choice of allowing editing (**Can edit**). Give an **expiration date** and click on **Apply**.

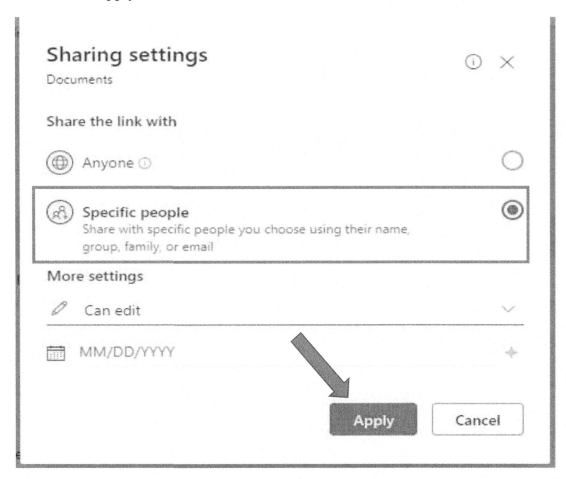

- For the **To** field, input the email addresses of the specific targets. If there is a need, attach a message.

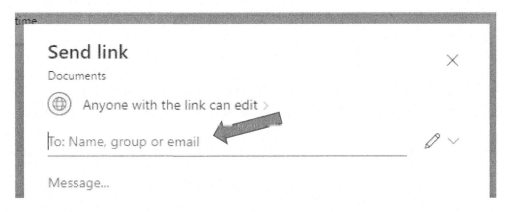

- Click **Send**.

Finding Shared Files

To find shared files on Microsoft OneDrive, follow these steps:

- Sign in to your OneDrive account.

- On the left-hand side of the screen, click on **Shared** to view all files and folders that have been shared with you.

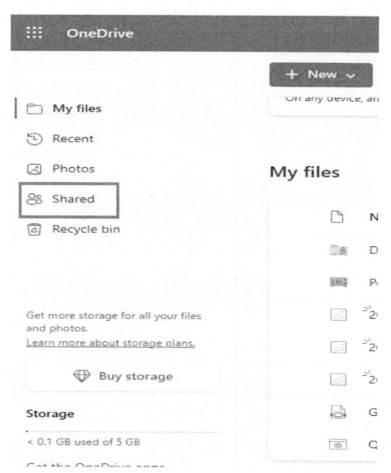

- You can filter the list by clicking on **Shared with you** or **Shared by you** to view files that have been shared by a specific person or shared with a specific person.

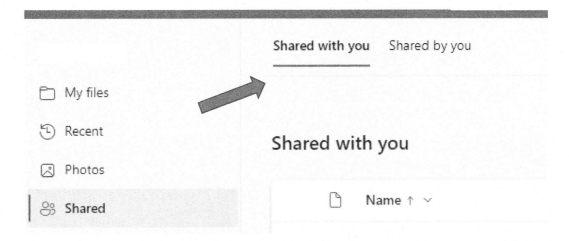

- You can also sort the list by name, date, or file type by clicking on **Sort**.

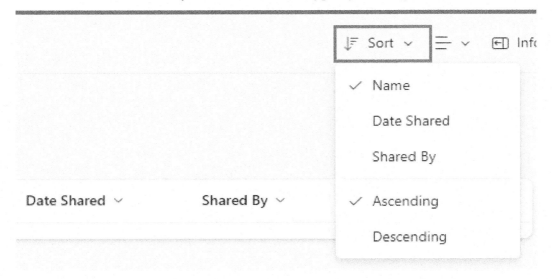

- To view the shared file, click on it. If the file is in a folder, click on the folder to open it and then click on the file.

- If you are also finding it difficult to locate desired file, use the search tool. There are available options, also, to filter search queries.

Embedding Files

Having a blog or website? Easily embed photos, documents, and other files in a quick manner with Microsoft OneDrive.

- Sign in to your Microsoft OneDrive account.

- Select the file to be embedded.

- Click on **Embed** from the list of options displayed, or click on the **ellipsis (...)** at the top of the page. Go to **Embed**.

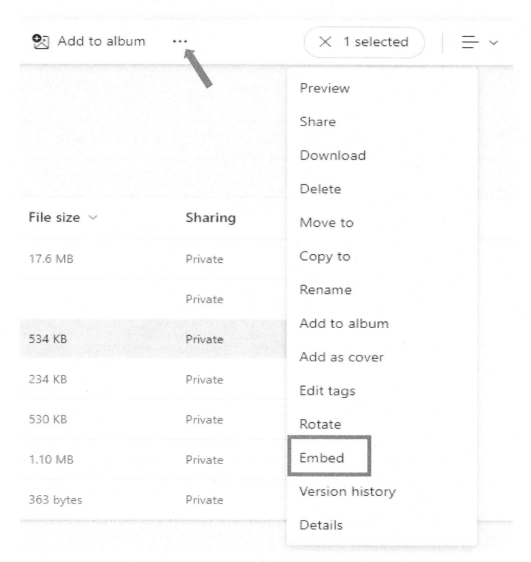

- Then click **Generate**.

- A link will be generated.

- Copy and paste the **URL** and use it on your website or blog.

When someone views your website or blog, they'll be able to see and interact with the embedded file without having to download it. This can be a convenient way to share files and collaborate on documents without sending them back and forth through email.

Saving Office Files to Microsoft OneDrive

- Open the Office file you want to save to OneDrive.

- Click on the **File** tab in the upper left corner of the window.

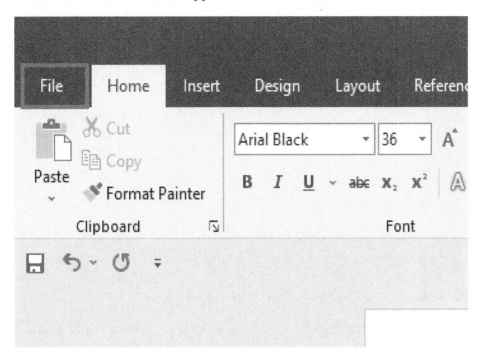

- Click **Save As** in the menu on the left side of the window.

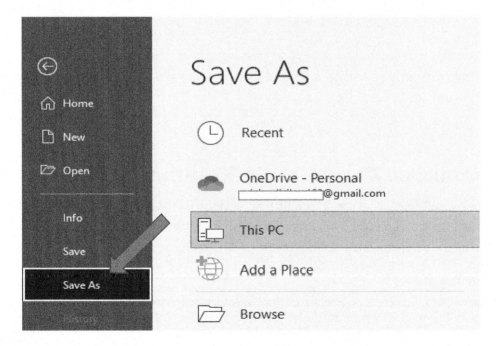

- Choose **OneDrive** as the location to save the file.

- Choose the folder within OneDrive where you want to save the file or create a new folder if needed.

- Name the file and choose the file type if necessary.

- Click **Save** to save the file to OneDrive.

Once the file is saved to OneDrive, access it from any device with an internet connection by logging into your OneDrive account. You can also share the file with others by giving them permission to access it.

Collaborating on Documents in Real-time

Microsoft Office and OneDrive can be integrated with different people working or collaborating on a Word document, Excel, or PowerPoint. Real-time collaboration is one effective way to save time, and the ideal way is to share documents through OneDrive.

Sharing your Document

- To share the word document, go to the ribbon and click **Share**.

- Follow the prompts and select a person you want to share the document with. Input the email address.

- Input a message, although optional. Then click Share.

- **Choose the Collaboration Level**

- Once you've shared the document, you can choose the collaboration level. People can be allowed to edit the document, or you restrict them to just viewing it.

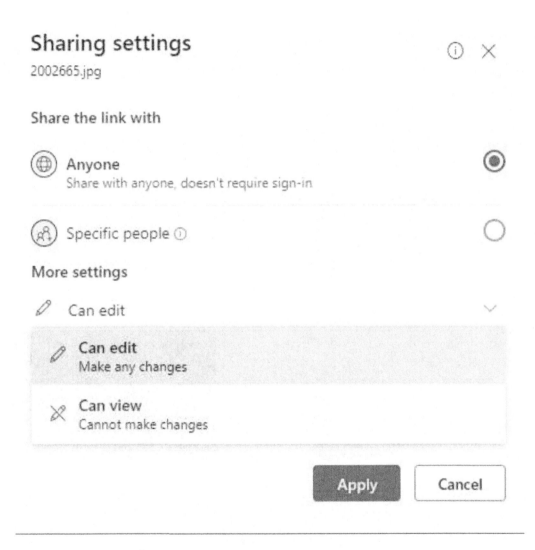

Edits can be made in real time. Collaborating on Word using the web is one good experience as you'll be able to see the changes as they happen, and you can also make edits to the document at the same time.

Track/Review Changes

In order to keep track of changes, go to **Review**, then **Track changes**.

To review any change, put the cursor before any changes made and pick either **Accept**, to retain the change, or **Reject**, to remove changes.

Creating Photo Album

The Microsoft OneDrive photo album presents your photos in a well-organized manner. Creating one is quite easy.

- Open Microsoft OneDrive.

- Click on the **Photos** option seen on the left pane.

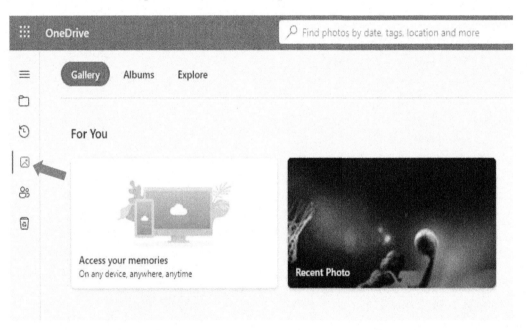

- Go to **Album** tab and click **Create a new album**.

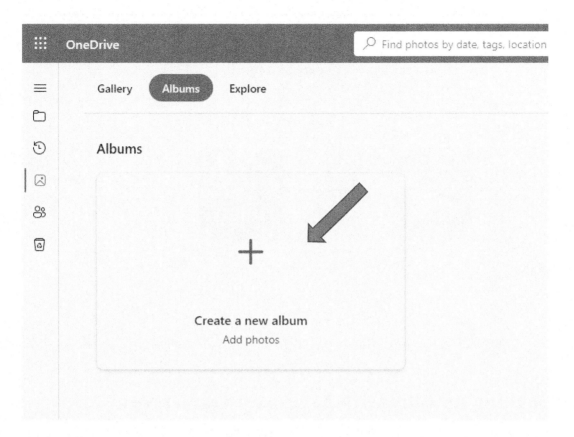

- Create a desired name for the album.

ONEDRIVE ALBUM

Add photos

- After naming, click **Add photos**.

- Select photos and click on **Create album**.

Backing up Files with Microsoft OneDrive

Backing up your files with OneDrive offers protection and availability across all means of access.

- Go to the OneDrive icon on the taskbar and double-click. You may also need to click the arrow pointing upwards to access the icon.

- Click on the **Help & Settings** option. Go to **Settings.**

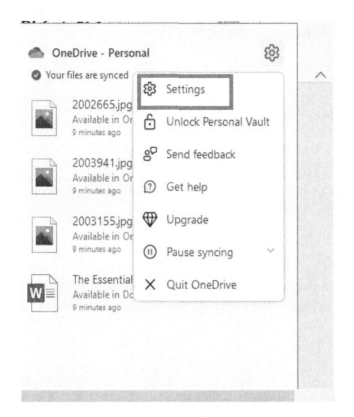

- Click on **Backup** from the different tabs seen at the top of the window.

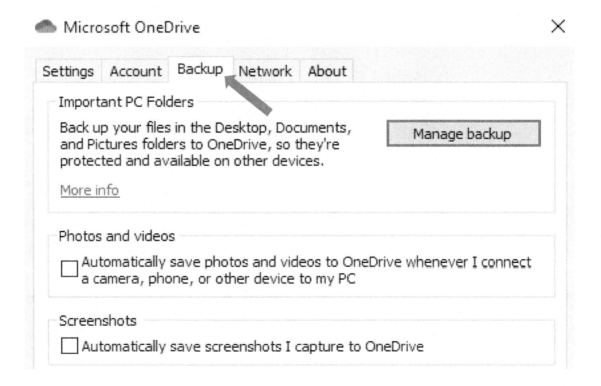

- Go to **Manage backup** following the Important PC Folder.

- The Microsoft OneDrive then displays **Manage folder backup**. Make a selection of the folders to be backed up, for example, the Desktop, Documents, and Pictures folders.

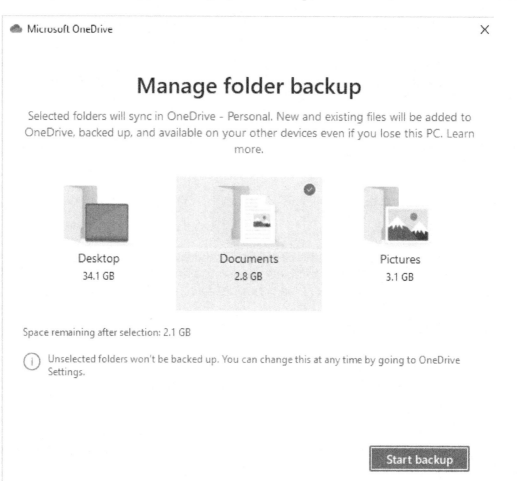

- Click on **Start backup**.

OneDrive will kickstart the cloud backup process and keep a copy on the device.

Accessing Recent Activities on OneDrive

To access recent activities on OneDrive, you can follow these steps:

- Go to the OneDrive website and sign in with your Microsoft account.

- Click on the **Recent** option in the left-hand sidebar menu.

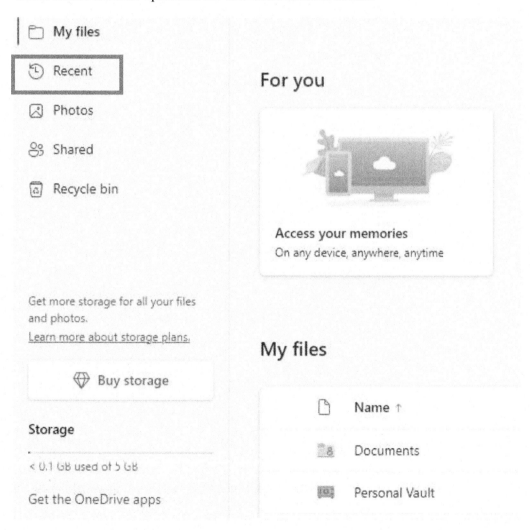

- This will display a list of your most recent activities on OneDrive, such as files you've uploaded or edited, folders you've created or deleted, and shared items.

- To see more details about a specific activity, hover over it and click on the **ellipsis (...)** that appears on the right side. This will give you options to view details, open the file, or manage sharing settings.

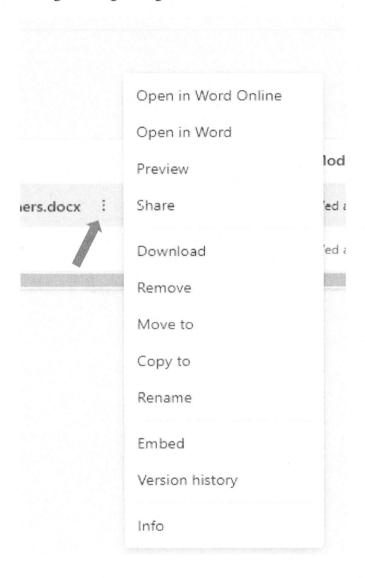

- You can also use the search bar at the top of the page to search for specific files or activities.

Creation of Word, Excel, and PowerPoint from OneDrive

To create Word, Excel, and PowerPoint documents from OneDrive, you can follow these steps:

- Sign in to your OneDrive account on your preferred web browser.

- Once you are logged in, click the **New** button on the left-hand side of the screen.

- From the drop-down menu, select the type of document you want to create (Word, Excel, or PowerPoint).

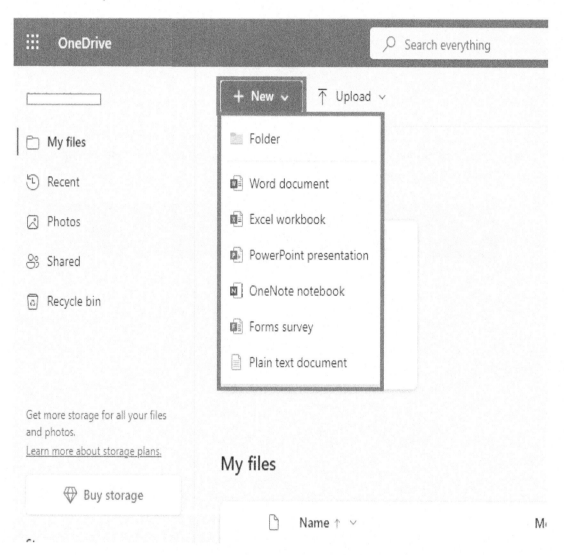

- A new document will open in your browser. (Ms. Word)

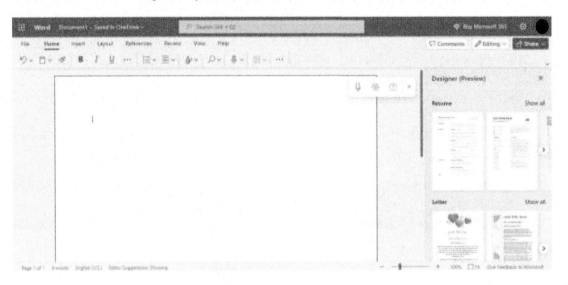

- Give your document a name by clicking on the default name at the top of the screen and typing in the name you want.

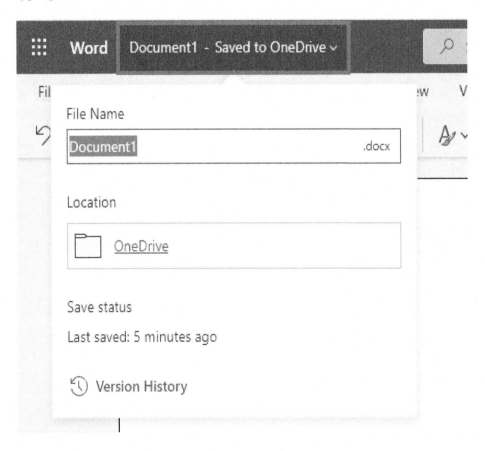

- Start editing your document using the toolbar at the top of the screen. You can add text, images, tables, charts, and more.

- Once you are done editing, click on the **File** menu at the top-left corner of the screen.

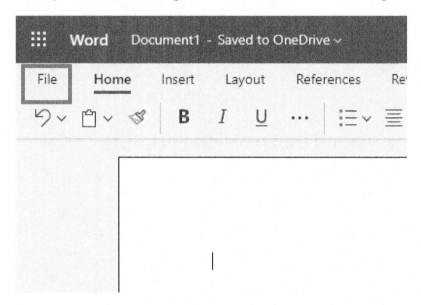

- From the drop-down menu, you can save your document, download it, or share it with others by sending them a link or inviting them to collaborate.

File Restoration Using OneDrive Recycle Bin

One of the useful features of OneDrive is its ability to restore files that have been deleted or lost. Here's how you can restore files using Microsoft OneDrive:

- Log in to your OneDrive account using your Microsoft credentials.

- Click on the **Recycle bin** icon on the left-hand panel of the OneDrive interface. This will display all the files and folders deleted from your OneDrive storage.

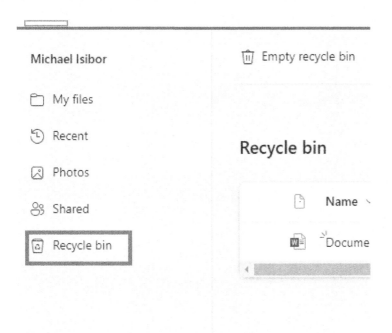

- Select the files or folders that you want to restore. You can select multiple files and folders by holding down the **Ctrl** key on your keyboard and clicking each item.

- Once you have selected the files and folders you want to restore, click the **Restore** button from the list or at the top of the interface.

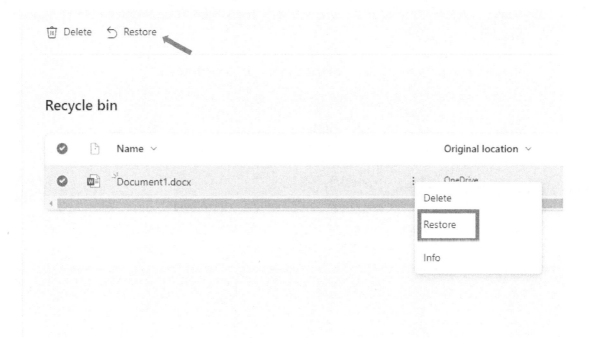

- OneDrive will restore the selected files and folders.

OneDrive will restore the files and folders to their original location in your OneDrive storage. If the files were in a folder that you deleted, OneDrive will recreate the folder and restore the files to it.

Restore Files on OneDrive

The restore option is available for files already deleted, corrupted, overwritten, or affected by malware. Files are allowed to be restored within a 30-day time frame and are previously located in OneDrive.

- After signing in, click on **Settings** and go to **Options**.

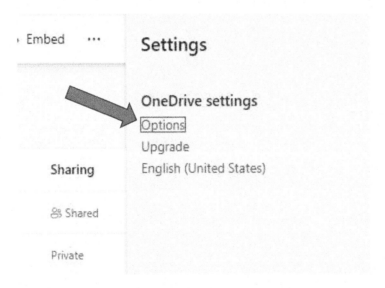

- **Restore your OneDrive**. Microsoft support access provides a list of options to restore files. Restore your OneDrive.

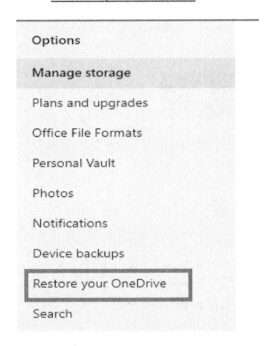

- Apart from making use of the Recycle bin, you will have the option to select how far back you want the restoration to occur using **Version history**.

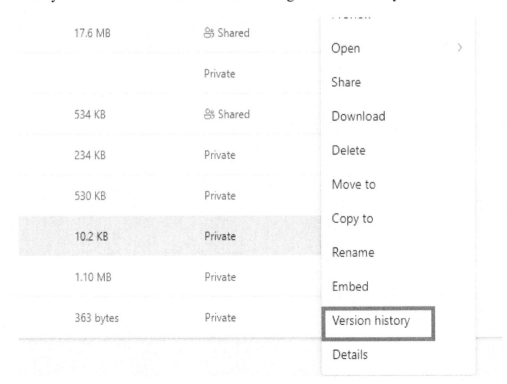

- You can pick a date or go to the bottom of the page to check all the changes made previously and choose from when you want the restoration, and also files that may be affected.

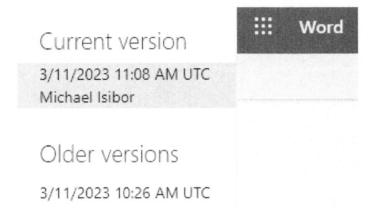

- Click on the **date and time** of the older version to be restored.

- Click **Restore** or **Download**.

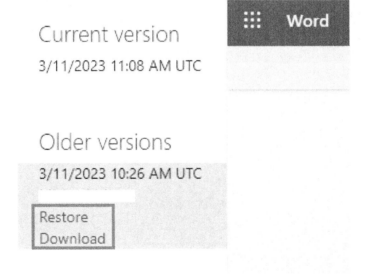

Turn Off Automatic Sync

To turn off automatic sync on Microsoft OneDrive, you can follow these steps:

- Click the OneDrive icon in the system tray at your screen's bottom right-hand corner.

- Click on the gear icon and then select **Settings**.

- In the **Account** tab, click on the **Choose folders** option.

- This will open a dialog box. Uncheck the box next to **Make all files available**.

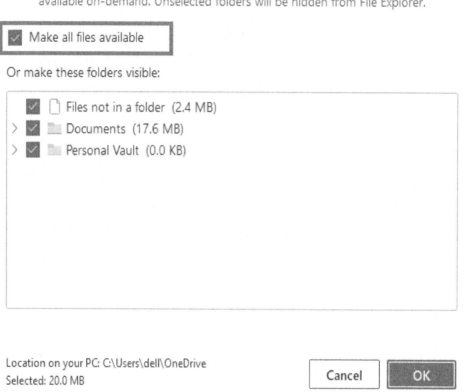

- Click on **OK** to save the changes.

- Once you turn off automatic sync, your files will no longer be automatically synced to OneDrive. You can still manually upload and download files to and from OneDrive as needed.

CHAPTER FOUR

OneDrive on Your Mobile Devices

OneDrive is also available for mobile devices to help you get access to files on the go. The app is available for iOS and Android devices.

Getting Started/Installation

For iOS devices:

- Go to the App Store on your iPhone or iPad.

- Search for the Microsoft OneDrive app using the search bar

- After seeing the OneDrive app, tap the **Get** button close to the app to kickstart the download.

- After the download/installation, open the app and sign in with your Microsoft account.

For Android devices:

- Make use of the Google Play Store app on your device.

- Go to Play Store and search for Microsoft OneDrive on the search bar.

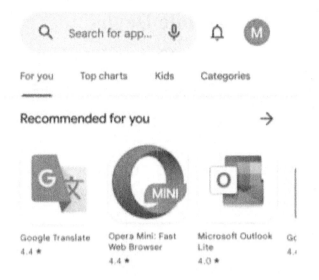

- Tap on the **Install** option close to the app.

- After installation, open the Microsoft OneDrive app and sign in with your Microsoft account.

There may be a need to grant permission to the app to access your device's storage, coupled with other permissions, during the installation process.

Setting Up OneDrive on Your Mobile Device

- Download the OneDrive app from the Google Play Store or App Store.

- On opening the app, you'll be prompted to choose whether to allow OneDrive to access your device's files and media. Select **Allow** if you want to upload files from your device to OneDrive and access your OneDrive files on your device.

- Sign in with your Microsoft account or create a new one if you don't already have one.

Protect your files and access them anywhere

SIGN IN

No account? Create one!

Skip to my photos

- Enter your email and password associated with the account.

 Microsoft

Sign in

Enter your work, school or personal Microsoft account

Email or phone	

- Automatically back up photos and videos from your device to OneDrive by selecting **Turn on camera backup** when prompted. You can skip this step and manually upload photos and videos later.

Save your memories

Turn on camera backup to back up all your photos
and videos and access them on any device.

Photos and videos only back up over Wi-Fi.

TURN ON CAMERA BACKUP

LATER

- Once you're finished setting up, you can now use OneDrive on your device.

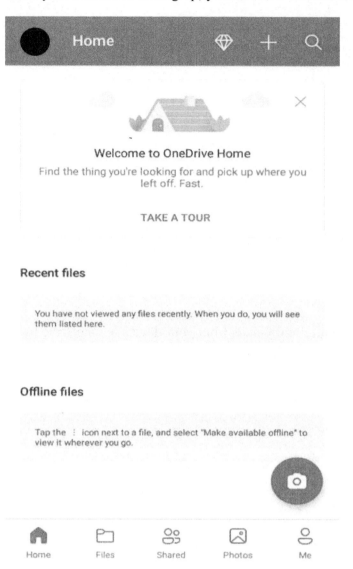

Syncing Your OneDrive Files to Your Mobile Device

- Launch the OneDrive app on your mobile device.

- Make sure you are signed in with your Microsoft account.

- By default, OneDrive will sync all the files and folders stored in your OneDrive account to your mobile device.

- If you want to change which files and folders are synced, go to **Files**.

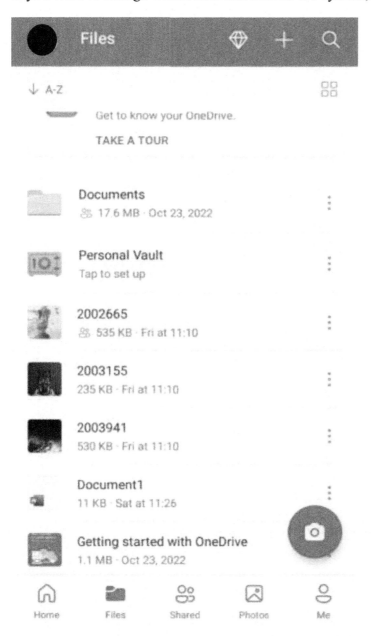

- Tap the three-dot icon next to the file or folder and select **Make available offline**.

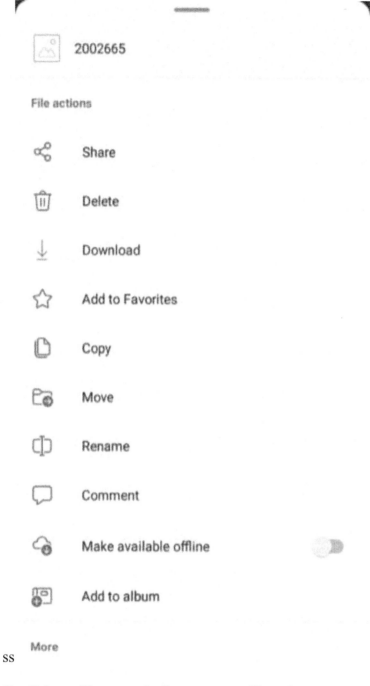

2002665

File actions

Share

Delete

Download

Add to Favorites

Copy

Move

Rename

Comment

Make available offline

Add to album

More

ss

- OneDrive will automatically sync your files whenever you make changes to them on your mobile device or another device connected to your OneDrive account.

- You can adjust your sync settings by clicking **Me** and selecting **Settings**.

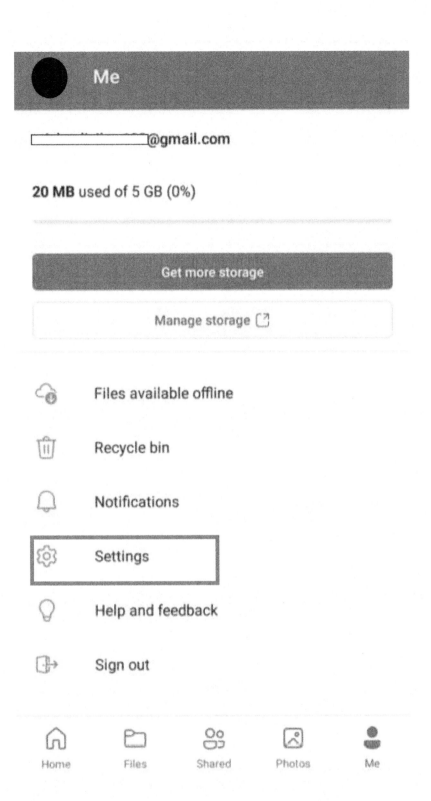

Me

[redacted]@gmail.com

20 MB used of 5 GB (0%)

Get more storage

Manage storage ↗

Files available offline

Recycle bin

Notifications

Settings

Help and feedback

Sign out

Home   Files   Shared   Photos   Me

- From here, you can choose to sync your files when connected to Wi-Fi or mobile data and adjust other settings to optimize your OneDrive experience on your device.

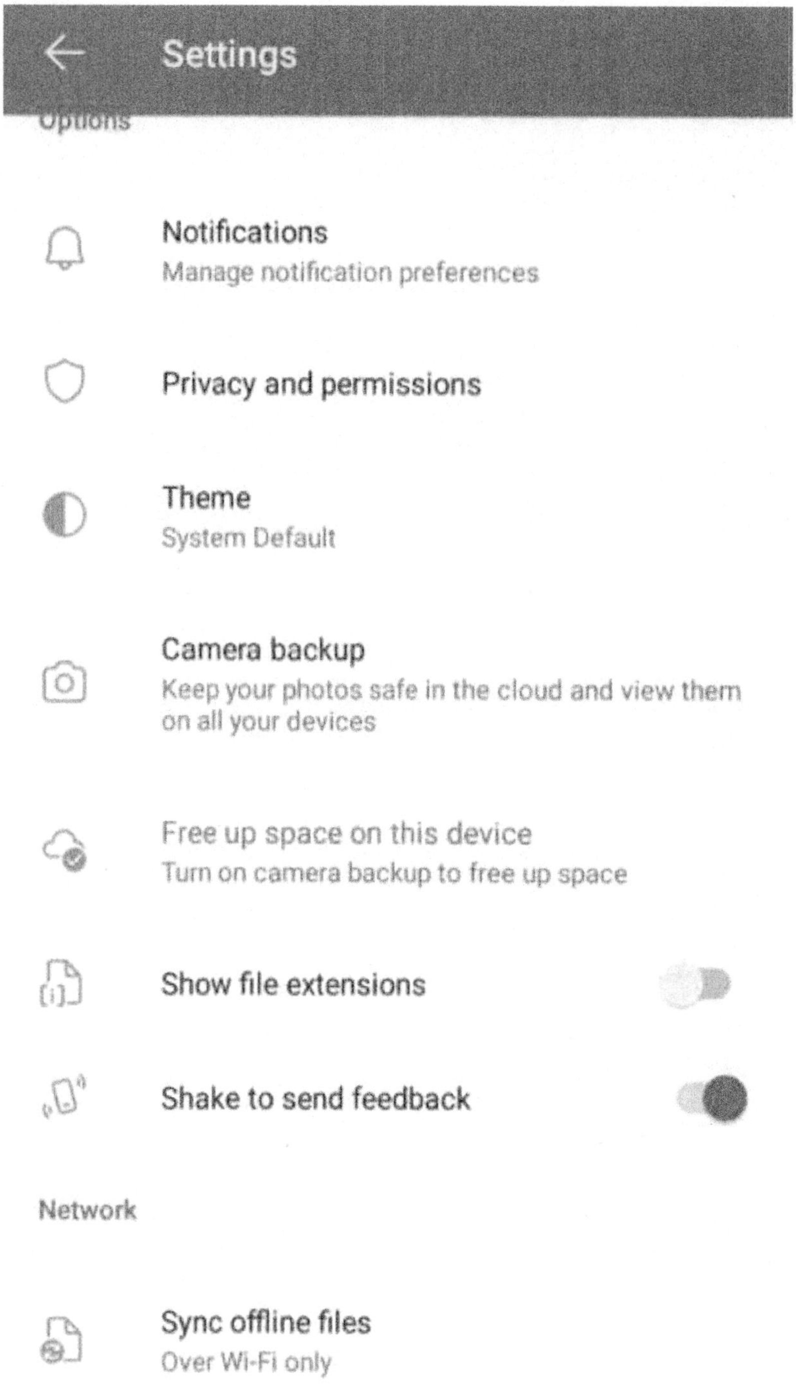

Options

Notifications
Manage notification preferences

Privacy and permissions

Theme
System Default

Camera backup
Keep your photos safe in the cloud and view them
on all your devices

Free up space on this device
Turn on camera backup to free up space

Show file extensions

Shake to send feedback

Network

Sync offline files
Over Wi-Fi only

86

Uploading Files to OneDrive

- Open the OneDrive app on your device.

- Tap the + icon at the top of the screen.

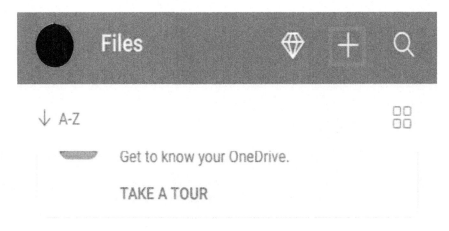

- Select **Upload** from the menu that appears.

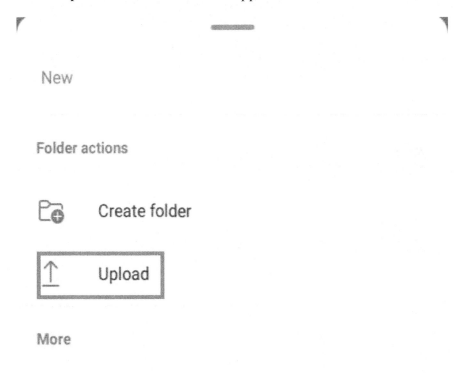

- Find the file you want to upload and select it.

- If you want to upload multiple files, tap and hold the first file and then tap on any additional files you want to upload.

- Once you've selected all the files you want to upload, open the file(s), and the uploading process will begin.

- Once the upload is complete, the file will be available in OneDrive on all your devices, including your computer.

Sharing Files on OneDrive

If you want to share files from OneDrive on your mobile device, here are the steps to follow:

- Open the OneDrive app on your mobile device.

- Navigate to the file you want to share.

- Tap and hold on the file to select it and select the **Share** button.

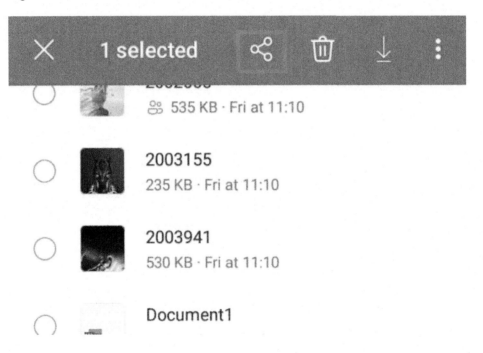

- Choose the app or service you want to use to share the file. Make a choice from options like email, messaging apps, social media, or even other cloud storage services.

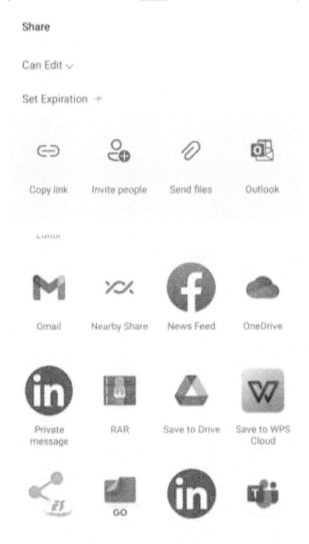

- Follow the prompts to complete the sharing process.

You can also share a link to a file stored on OneDrive. To do this:

- Tap and hold on the file to select it.

- Tap the **Share** button.

- Tap **Copy link**.

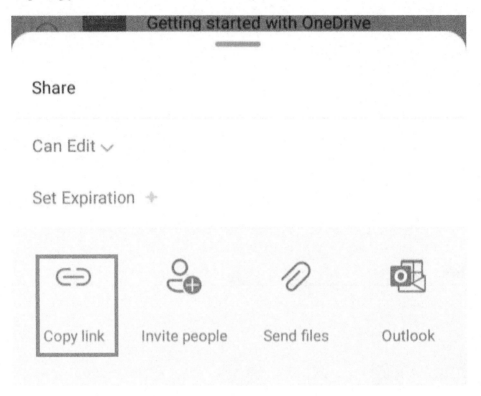

- Paste the link wherever you want to share it, like in an email or a messaging app.

Note that the steps above may vary slightly depending on your mobile device and operating system.

Access OneDrive Files Offline on your Mobile Device

- Open the OneDrive app on your device.

- Find the file or folder you want to access offline.

- Tap the ellipse (three dots) icon next to the file or folder.

- Select **Make available offline** from the options.

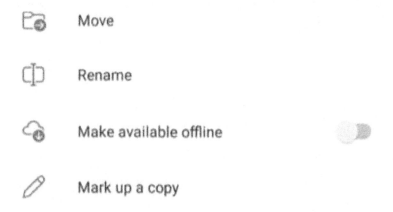

- The file or folder will begin downloading to your device. This can be seen from your notification bar.

- Also, a checkmark will appear next to it to indicate it is available offline.

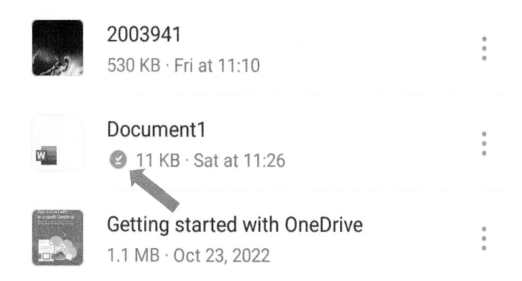

- Once you have downloaded the files or folders you need, you can access them offline by opening the OneDrive app and going to the Offline tab. Any files or folders you have made available offline will be listed here and can be accessed without an internet connection.

Offline files

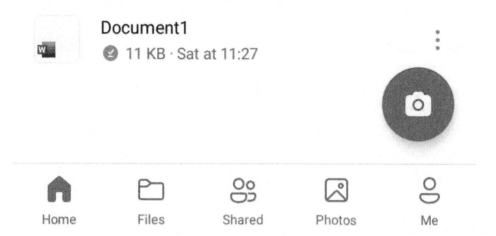

Document1

11 KB · Sat at 11:27

Home   Files   Shared   Photos   Me

CHAPTER FIVE

Integrating OneDrive with Other Applications

Integrating OneDrive with other applications has become a quintessential aspect of modern computing. With its cloud-based storage capabilities, OneDrive enables users to access their files and folders anywhere and on any device. However, to fully leverage its potential, OneDrive must be seamlessly integrated with other applications that are commonly used in the digital ecosystem.

Connecting OneDrive with Microsoft Office

Connecting OneDrive with Microsoft Office allows you to easily access and save files from OneDrive within Office applications like Word, Excel, and PowerPoint.

Here's how to connect OneDrive with Microsoft Office:

- Open any Office application such as Word, Excel, or PowerPoint.

- Click on the **File** tab in the upper left-hand corner of the application.

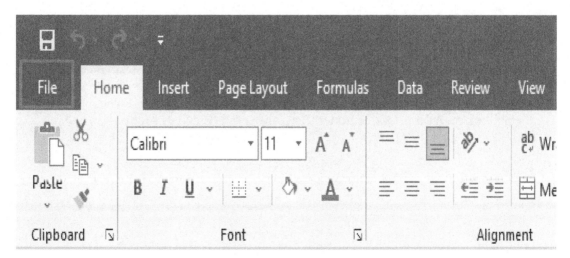

- Click on **Account** in the left-hand menu.

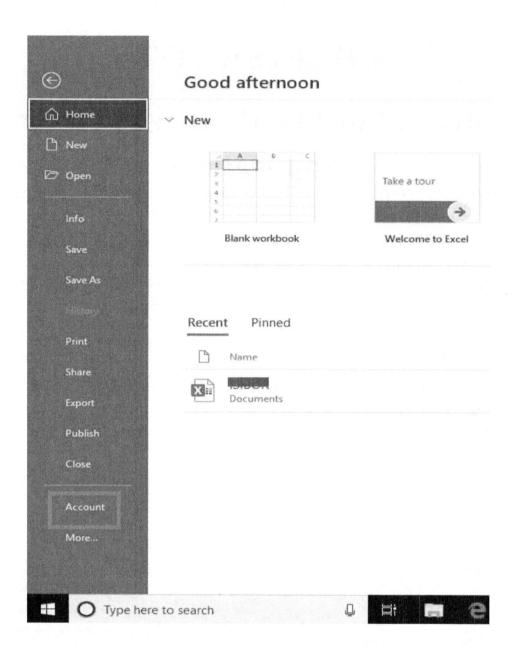

- Click on **Add** a service under the **Connected Services** section.

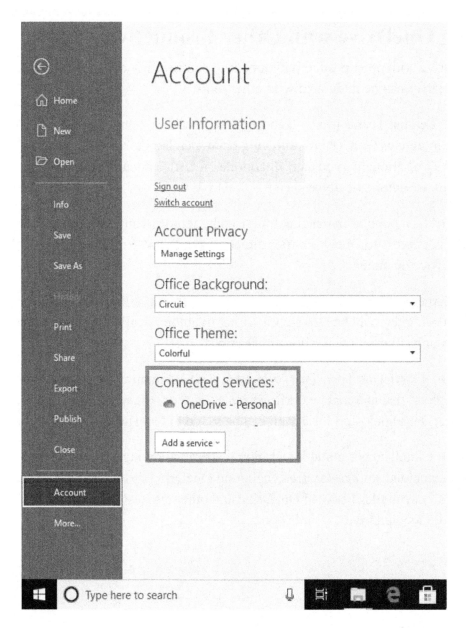

- Select OneDrive from the list of available services.

- Enter your Microsoft account credentials to sign in to OneDrive.

- Follow the prompts to complete the setup process

Once you have connected OneDrive with Microsoft Office, you will see a OneDrive option when you click the **Save As** or **Open** buttons within Office applications. You can then easily access and save files to your OneDrive account from within Office applications.

Integrating OneDrive with Other Productivity Tools

Integrating OneDrive with other productivity tools can significantly enhance your workflow and productivity. OneDrive can be integrated with other tools:

- **Microsoft Teams**: Teams is a collaboration tool enabling teams to work remotely. OneDrive integrates with Teams, allowing team members to access, share, and edit files in real time. Additionally, you can collaborate on Office documents within Teams, and the changes are automatically synced to OneDrive.

- **Slack**: Slack is a popular messaging tool used by remote teams. On integration, users can share and get access to OneDrive files directly from Slack. Collaboration can also be done on Office documents.

- **Zapier**: Zapier is a tool that enables users to automate repetitive tasks between different apps. You can integrate OneDrive with Zapier to automatically save files to OneDrive from other apps like Gmail, Trello, and Dropbox.

- **IFTTT**: IFTTT (If This Then That) is another web automation tool that allows you to create "applets" that automate workflows between different apps. Files from other apps like Twitter, Facebook, and Instagram can be saved to OneDrive on integration.

- **CloudHQ**: CloudHQ is a cloud integration platform allowing you to sync and backup files between cloud storage services, including OneDrive. With CloudHQ, you can automatically sync files between OneDrive and other cloud storage services, such as Dropbox or Google Drive.

CHAPTER SIX

OneDrive Tips and Tricks

Making Uploads Using Phone Camera

To make uploads using your phone's camera, follow these steps:

- Open the OneDrive app on your phone.

- Tap the + icon at the top of the screen.

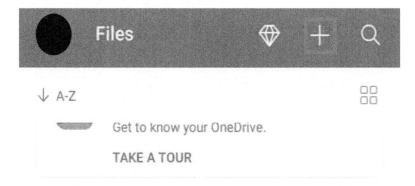

- Select **Take a Photo** from the options.

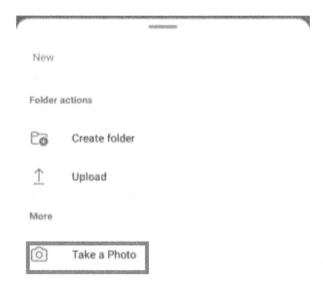

- Point your phone's camera at the item you want to upload.

- Tap the **capture** button to take the photo.

- Review the photo to make sure it's what you want to upload.

- If you're satisfied, proceed to begin the upload process.

- Wait for the upload to finish. The time it takes will depend on the size of the file and the speed of your internet connection.

Once the upload is complete, you'll be able to access your photo or video from any device connected to your OneDrive account.

The upload process may differ slightly depending on your device and the version of the OneDrive app you're using. However, the general steps outlined above should work for most users.

Scanning of Documents

Scanning can become quite handy, especially in keeping track of important documents. With the Microsoft OneDrive cloud storage, your documents or receipts are automatically synced and can be accessed from anywhere.

To scan documents using Microsoft OneDrive, you can follow these steps:

- Open the OneDrive app on your mobile device or computer.

- Click or tap on the + icon at the bottom of the screen to create a new file or folder.

- Choose **Scan** from the list of options.

- Align your document within the frame on your screen.

- Click or tap on the capture button to take a picture of the document.

- If needed, you can take additional pictures of different pages of the same document.

- Once you've finished scanning, click or tap on the **Done** button. Save document.

- The scanned document will be saved to your OneDrive account.

Microsoft Power Automate with OneDrive

Microsoft Power Automate, formerly Microsoft Flow, is a cloud-based service that allows users to create automated workflows between various applications and services. Power Automate can automate tasks related to OneDrive, such as creating a new folder, uploading files, and sending notifications when files are updated.

The flow system works in the way of automating configured triggers to carry out actions. This service is available to Office 365 users, and tasks can be automated amongst several applications such as SharePoint, Excel, Azure, Outlook, Online Office, Gmail, Twitter, YouTube, and others.

Here are the steps to use Microsoft Power Automate with OneDrive:

- On getting access to the website, you can opt-in using the **Start free** or **Buy now** options.

- Sign in to your <u>Microsoft Power Automate</u> account. Select country and click **Get started**.

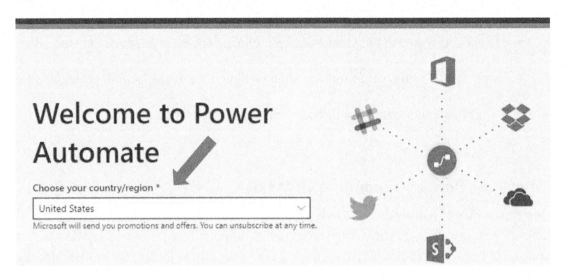

- Click on the **Create** button on the top navigation bar.

- Select **Start with a template** or **Build your own** from the list of options.

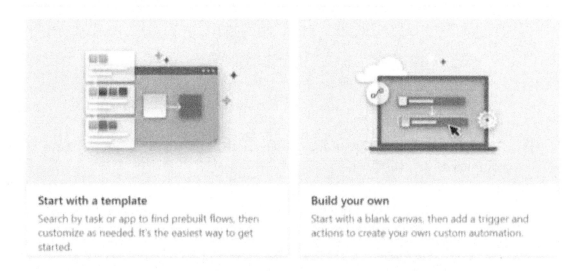

Start with a template

Search by task or app to find prebuilt flows, then customize as needed. It's the easiest way to get started.

Build your own

Start with a blank canvas, then add a trigger and actions to create your own custom automation.

- Choose the trigger for the workflow. Use the **Filter by** or **search by keywords**. Select your desired template. For example, you can choose "Notify and Email when a new file is uploaded to OneDrive" as the trigger.

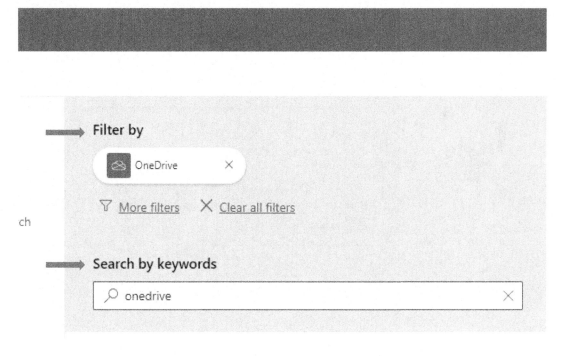

- Give a name to your flow and sign in to your OneDrive account.

Flow name

Notify and Email when a new file is uploaded to OneDrive

Sign in *

Power Automate uses your credentials to sign in and create connections. A green check means you're ready to go.

OneDrive   Sign in

- Allow OneDrive to access information. Click **Next** after the signing-in has been completed.

- Carry out necessary configurations

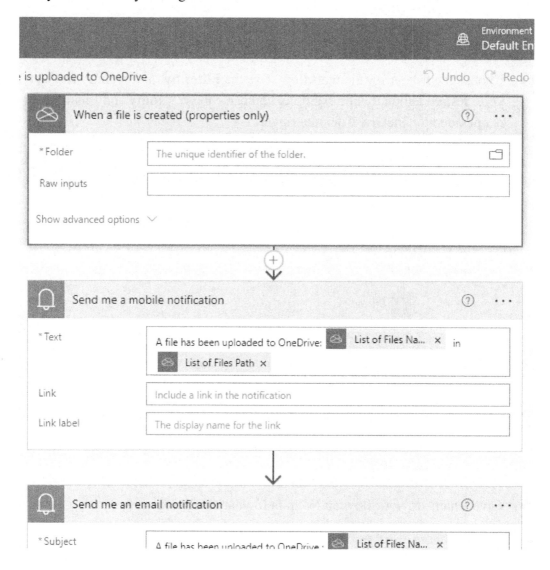

- You can add another step to accompany your selected template. Click on **New step**.

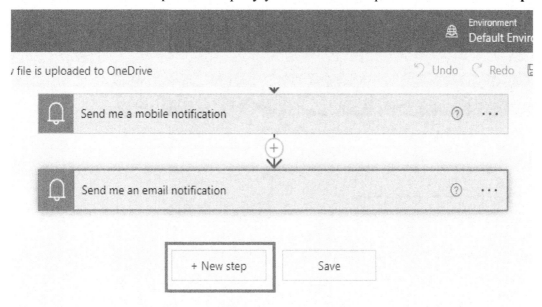

- Choose from the list of operations.

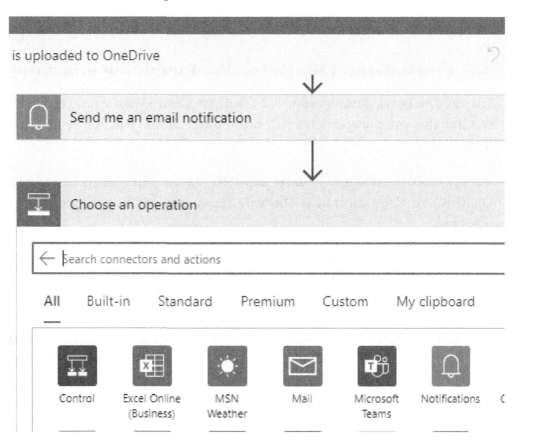

- Click Save.

The **Flow Checker** on the dashboard enables you to identify errors or warnings, while the **Test** option allows you to see instant operations.

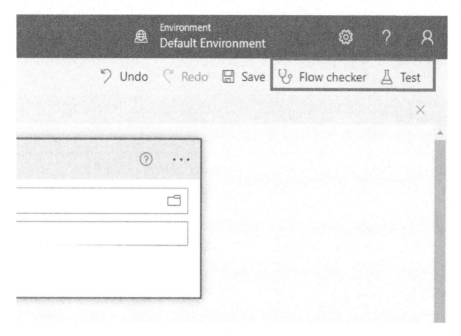

Tips for Optimizing OneDrive Performance and Speed

- **Use the OneDrive desktop app**: The OneDrive desktop app syncs your files with the cloud so that you can access them from anywhere. It also makes it faster to upload and download files.

- **Pause OneDrive syncing**: If you're experiencing slow internet speeds, you can pause OneDrive syncing temporarily. This will free up bandwidth and allow you to perform other tasks.

- **Optimize OneDrive settings**: You can optimize OneDrive settings to improve performance. For example, you can choose which folders to sync, set upload and download limits, and enable automatic uploads.

- **Use selective sync**: If you have a large number of files in OneDrive, you can use selective sync to only sync the files you need. This can help speed up syncing and reduce storage usage.

- **Use the OneDrive web interface**: If you're not near your synced device, you can use the OneDrive web interface to access your files. This interface is useful when you need to access files quickly and can also help reduce the load on your device.

- **Clear the OneDrive cache**: OneDrive caches files to speed up syncing. However, the cache can become bloated over time and slow down syncing. Clear the OneDrive cache to free up space and improve performance.

- **Monitor OneDrive activity**: Make use of the OneDrive activity center to monitor file uploads and downloads. Effective monitoring can help you identify any issues and improve performance.

- **Keep your device up to date:** Ensure that your device is up to date with the latest updates and patches to improve performance.

- **Consider upgrading your internet plan**: If you're experiencing slow internet speeds, upgrade your internet plan. This can help improve upload and download speeds, speeding up OneDrive syncing.

CHAPTER SEVEN

Troubleshooting and Maintenance

While OneDrive is generally a reliable service coming as a great solution to any issue relating to data storage, it may encounter errors and issues that can affect its functionality, thus affecting users' experience.

Common OneDrive issues and solutions

There are some common issues associated with Microsoft OneDrive.

Syncing Issues with OneDrive

It is actually one of the problems encountered mostly by users as files cannot be synced across all platforms, especially with the web account. In this case, files are not syncing with the cloud account, so forcing the app to sync manually is the ideal solution. The easy solution is to restart the app after closing it.

- To do this, go to the Microsoft OneDrive icon on the taskbar or system tray. Right-click on it, head to the gear or Settings icon and select **Quit OneDrive**. This will shut down the app.

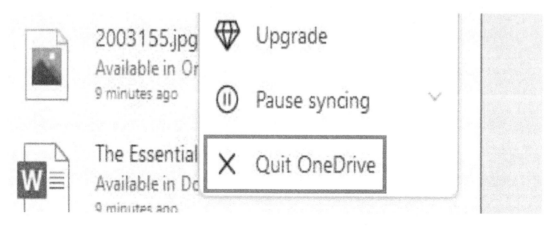

- Go to the search bar or start menu and click on the OneDrive app. The app is relaunched, and the syncing process restarted.

- For other means of solution, ensure you have a stable internet connection. OneDrive requires a reliable internet connection to sync your files.

- Check your storage limit, as OneDrive comes with a storage limit. If you have reached your storage limit, you won't be able to sync any new files. You can check your OneDrive storage limit by going to the OneDrive website.

- Make sure that you have the latest version of OneDrive installed. Check for updates in the app store or on the OneDrive website.

No OneDrive Icon on the Computer

You might have probably searched your computer for the OneDrive icon, and pinpointing the exact location is seemingly impossible. Well, this might have happened for several reasons, but the solution isn't far-fetched. If there is no icon on the taskbar:

- Go to the taskbar, right-click, and select **Taskbar Settings** from the menu.

- On opening, go to **Notification area**. Click **Select which icons appear on the taskbar**.

Look for **Microsoft OneDrive** and toggle it on.

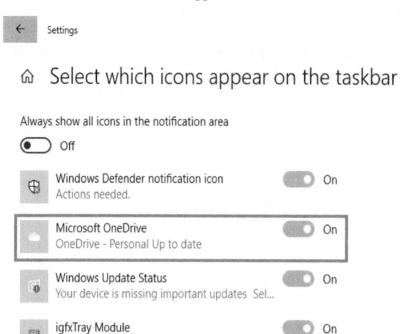

- If the OneDrive icon isn't still on display in File Explorer, there is a need to apply changes in the Windows registry.

- Applying changes to the registry should be done carefully. A mistake may alter the registry when editing, so ensure a backup of the entire registry before proceeding.

To make edits:

- Open the Run dialog box using **Win+R**.

- Input **Regedit** into the text space and click **OK**.

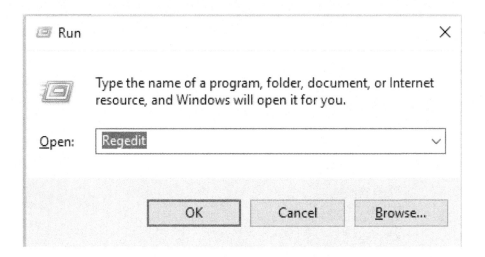

- Click **Yes** after the **User Account Control** opens.

- When the Editor window opens, expand HKEY_LOCAL_MACHINE >> SOFTWARE >> Policies >> Microsoft >> OneDrive.

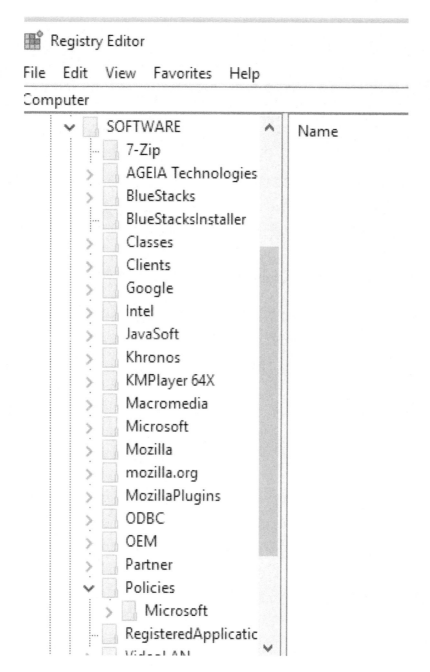

- Click the OneDrive key seen under Microsoft, and on the right side, double-click **DisableFileSyncNGSC** and input 0 into the Value Data box.

- Double-click also, on **DisableFileSync,** and type in 0 in the box.

- Reboot your computer after making the changes.

Missing OneDrive Files

Once files are successfully uploaded to OneDrive, they are less likely to be missing or go missing. There are chances that such a file might have been deleted, failed to sync successfully, or have been synced using a different or wrong account; the more reason such file cannot be seen.

When looking for a file, make use of the search feature. Log into your OneDrive account and type in the file name. If not found, check the Recycle bin. Also, ensure that where the file was synced is the appropriate account. Check others if you have multiple accounts.

"Upgrade Browser" Error

The "Upgrade Browser" error when using OneDrive usually indicates that your web browser is outdated and is no longer supported by OneDrive. You must update your web browser to a newer version to fix this error. Here are the steps you can follow:

- Determine which web browser you are using. OneDrive supports the latest versions of Microsoft Edge, Google Chrome, Mozilla Firefox, and Apple Safari.

- Check if you have the latest version of your web browser installed. To do this, go to your browser's settings or help menu and look for an option to check for updates.

- If there is an update available, install it and restart your browser.

- If your browser is up to date and you still see the "Upgrade Browser" error, try clearing your browser's cache and cookies. Clear cache or cookies in the settings or privacy section of your browser.

If none of the above steps works, try using a different web browser supported by OneDrive.

Difficulty Uploading Files on the Web

Difficulty uploading files may arise due to trying to upload a large file or selecting files simultaneously. There is a limit to the size of file while uploading. You are allowed ***a 15GB file limit at a time using a school account.

Also, the file path, with the name included, should not exceed 400 characters.

Ms. Word Files Not Opening on the Web

Microsoft OneDrive allows you to create and edit Word documents from its web interface. If you are finding it difficult:

- Go to the folder where the file was saved.

- Select file. Click on **Open**, then **Open in Word** from the options provided at the top.

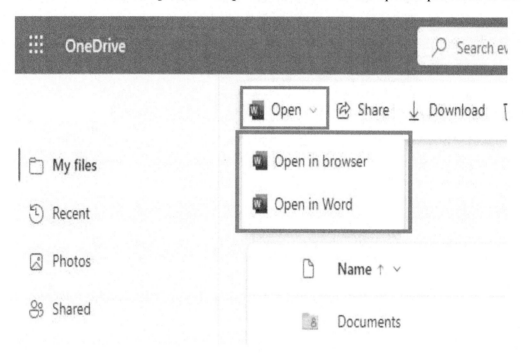

This will open the file in the online Word application anytime you need access.

OneDrive Automatically Paused on a PC

The process of syncing automatically pauses when the Battery Saver mode comes on. This is a means of preserving what's left of the battery life. To fix this, you need to turn off the Battery Saver.

- Launch the **Setting** app and click on **System**.

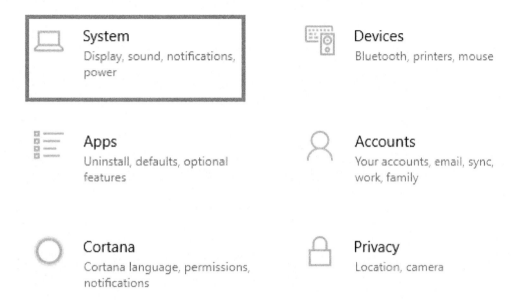

- On the left pane, scroll down and click on **Battery**.

- Then toggle off the **Battery saver** mode.

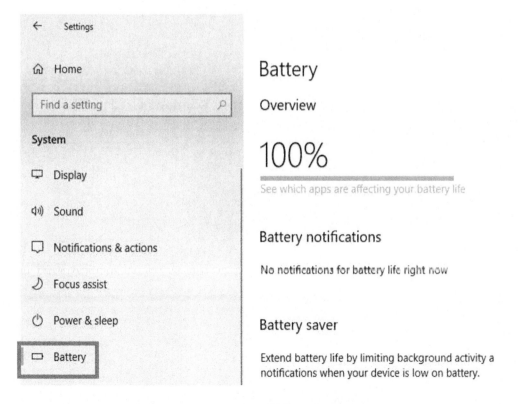

Error of Syncing a Different Account

This error comes up when trying to log in, usually when there is a change to an account's password. One way to get rid of this error is to clear cached credentials from your computer. To correct the error:

- Go to **Control Panel**. Click **User Account**.

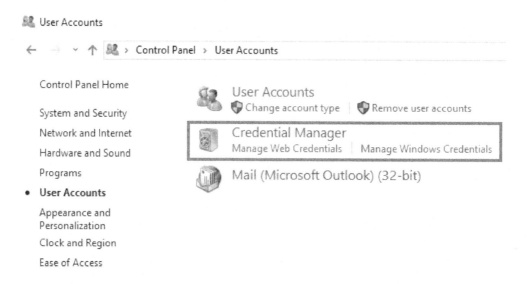

- On the page, select **Credential Manager**, then **Windows Credentials**.

- Look for OneDrive Cached Credentials and have them removed.

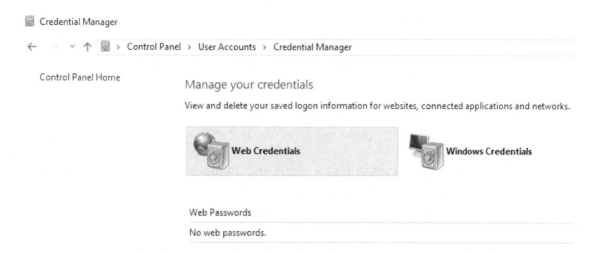

- Restart the OneDrive app and log in again.

- You can as well unlink the account and sign in.

Keeping OneDrive Up-to-date

To keep OneDrive up-to-date, you can follow these steps:

- Ensure you have the latest version of the OneDrive app installed on your device. You can check for updates in the Microsoft Store (on Windows) or the App Store (on Mac).

- Ensure that your device is connected to the internet and that you have a stable connection.

- Configure OneDrive settings to ensure files are automatically synced between your device and OneDrive. To do this, right-click the OneDrive icon in your system tray (on Windows) or menu bar (on Mac), and select Settings. From here, select the Account tab, and ensure that the Files On-Demand option is enabled. This ensures that all files and folders stored on OneDrive are available on your device without taking up unnecessary storage space.

- Once you've configured your OneDrive settings, it's important to regularly check for updates to ensure that you're running the latest version of the app. You can do this by periodically checking for updates in the Microsoft Store (on Windows) or the App Store (on Mac).

Securing your OneDrive Account

Microsoft OneDrive has, over time, ensured data protection and is regarded as one of the safest cloud storage services. However, OneDrive may be exposed to security risks that are potentially dangerous to cloud storage applications. The outcomes of these threats are data loss, corrupted files, or theft.

Securing your OneDrive account is important to protect your personal and confidential data. These are some tips to help you secure your OneDrive account:

- **Use a strong password**: Use a strong and unique password that includes both uppercase and lowercase letters, numbers, and symbols. Passwords in the form of names or birthdate are easily guessable; such should be avoided.

- **Enable two-factor authentication**: Two-factor authentication adds an extra layer of security to your account by requiring a code sent to your phone or email to access your account. It makes it harder for hackers to access your account even if they have your password.

- **Regularly update your security information**: Ensure that your email and phone number are up to date on your account. This is important if you need to recover your account or change your password.

- **Be careful with public computers**: Do not log in to your OneDrive account on a public computer, as the computer may have malware or spyware installed that could steal your login credentials. If you must use a public computer, ensure that you log out of your account and delete any stored login information.

- **Be cautious with links:** Avoid clicking on links in emails or messages that ask you to sign in to your OneDrive account. Always verify the URL and make sure it matches the official OneDrive website.

- **Use a trusted device**: Avoid logging in to your OneDrive account from a device that is not trusted. If you need to use a device that is not your own, use a private browsing session or clear your browsing history and cache after logging out of your account.

- **Monitor your account**: Regularly review your account activity to ensure no unusual activity exists. If you notice any suspicious activity, change your password immediately and report it to Microsoft.

Personal Vault

The Personal Vault provides a means of securing very important and delicate files, such as official documents, passports, tax, insurance information, and others, in such a way that access will not be easily compromised. It is an area within OneDrive that inculcates high-degree authentication or second-step identity verification such as face and fingerprint verification, PIN usage, or code sent to an email or phone number (through SMS). Files in Personal Vault are guaranteed an extra layer of security and are well secured in the incidence of unauthorized access to your OneDrive account.

With the Vault, you can store up to a good portion of the storage quota given to your OneDrive account, up to 1TB. When not in use for over 20mins, this area locks up automatically and with a two-factor authentication security system, making it a seemingly impenetrable fortress.

Setting Up the Personal Vault

- To get full access to the Vault, you will need to enable its operations from the **Settings** menu.

- On your OneDrive account, click on **Settings**, then **Options**.

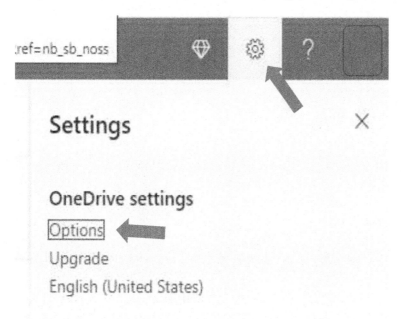

- Pick out the Personal Vault from the panel at the left side of the interface.

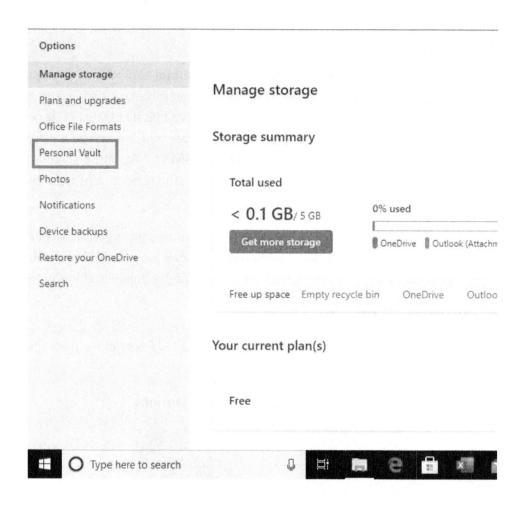

- After clicking, select **Enable**.

Personal Vault

Enable Personal Vault

Enable Personal Vault and keep your most important and sensitive files safe.

Enable

- You may be asked for verification to get access. To do this;

- Go to **Verify your identity**. You will be asked to verify through email or other means.

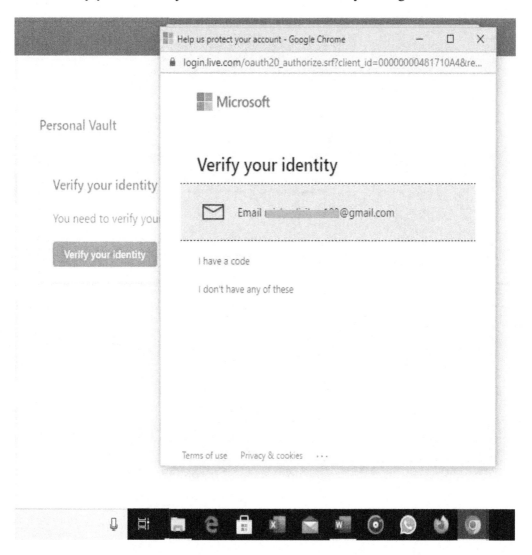

- After verification, you will be prompted of a successful activation of the Personal Vault.

- **Upload files or folders to Personal Vault**

- Go to OneDrive and sign in with your Microsoft account.

- Click on the **Personal Vault** folder.

es

	Name ↑ ∨	Modified ∨	File size ∨	Sharing
	Documents	11 hours ago	17.6 MB	ஃ Shared
	Personal Vault	15 minutes ago		Private
	2002665.jpg	4 days ago	534 KB	ஃ Shared

- If prompted, enter your two-step verification code or use your fingerprint or face recognition to access Personal Vault.

- Click on the **Upload** button in the top menu.

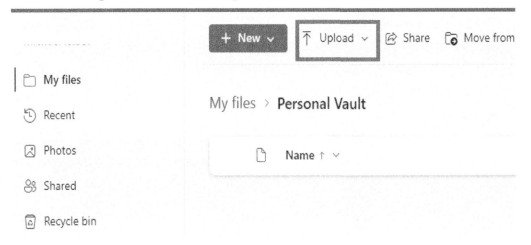

- Select the file or folder you want to upload from your computer.

- Click **Open** to start the upload.

- Wait for the upload to complete. The file or folder should now be stored securely in your Vault.

Move files to Personal Vault

Files in your OneDrive can be moved to the Personal Vault

To move files to Personal Vault on OneDrive, you can follow these steps:

- Sign in to your OneDrive account.

- Navigate to the file or folder you want to move to Personal Vault.

- Right-click on the file or folder and select **Move to** from the menu.

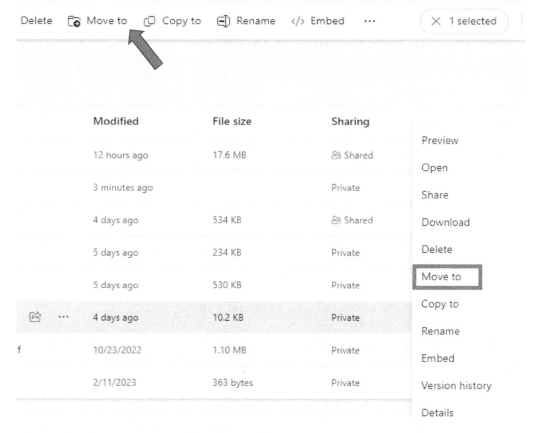

- Click on Personal Vault from the list of options.

- Click **Move to,** to get the file or folder into the Vault

Unlock your Personal Vault

The Personal Vault, when not in active use, locks itself automatically. Changes can be made to the period it will take for the automatic lock to kick in. To unlock it:

- Click on the Personal Vault option.

- You'll be prompted to enter a verification code sent to your email or OneDrive password. Enter the code or your password and click Sign in.

- Once verified, you should see your Vault. The icon will show an open vault. Click on it to get access.

Lock your Personal Vault

OneDrive automatically locks itself after a period of inactivity to protect your files from unauthorized access. By default, OneDrive will lock itself after 20 minutes, but this period can be adjusted.

When OneDrive locks itself, you need to sign in again by verifying your identity. This provides an extra layer of security and helps prevent anyone who might gain access to your computer from accessing your OneDrive files.

Disable Personal Vault

To disable Personal Vault in OneDrive, follow these steps:

- Go to Personal Vault under settings.

- Click **Disable** close to the **Disable personal vault** option.

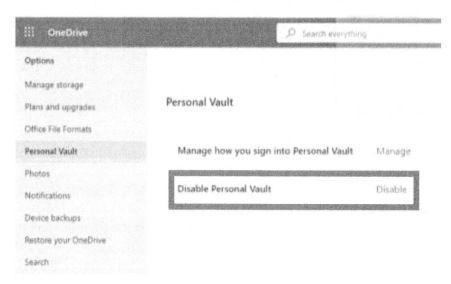

Disabling Personal Vault will lead to the deletion of all files in the Vault without option to restore.

Printed in Great Britain
by Amazon

39487976R00077